Praise for *Your Creative Mind*

"*Your Creative Mind* is a thought-provoking work that will challenge you and your business to think, to value the creativity that drives innovation, and, more importantly, to be committed to 'what's next?' and to understand how to achieve a successful outcome."

—Luanne Lenberg, senior vice president, Retail Properties, Penn-Florida Companies

"Students of business, and life, will find that this book stimulates their thinking. *Your Creative Mind* helps us understand how to harness the power of our individual, and collective, minds."

—Gerald Weber, CEO, Fast-Fix Jewelry & Watch Repair

Your *Creative* Mind

DISRUPT YOUR THINKING, ABANDON YOUR COMFORT ZONE, AND DEVELOP BOLD NEW STRATEGIES

SCOTT COCHRANE

YOUR CREATIVE MIND
TYPESET BY PERFECTYPE, NASHVILLE, TENN.
Cover design by Howard Grossman/12E Design
Printed in the U.S.A.

To order this title, please call toll-free 1-800-CAREER-1 (NJ and Canada: 201-848-0310) to order using VISA or MasterCard, or for further information on books from Career Press.

The Career Press, Inc.
12 Parish Drive
Wayne, NJ 07470
www.careerpress.com

Library of Congress Cataloging-in-Publication Data
CIP Data Available Upon Request.

ACKNOWLEDGMENTS

THIS BOOK WOULD NOT have been possible without the contribution of many people in a variety of ways, and I am endlessly grateful to all of them. Javier Carbajo stayed by my side during the entire process, fueling my creativity with his unique and meaningful insights. Maria del Moral enabled me to remain successfully focused on both the book and our business at the same time (wow!). Kevin Brown contributed volumes of stimulating research. Yolanda Harris helped me clarify my vision for the book and encouraged me to actually write it. Ganna Tiulkina created all of the artwork and was great fun to work with.

I would also like to thank my agent John Willig and all the people at Career Press and Brilliance for their tremendous support and flexibility. And finally, a very special thanks to my many valued clients throughout the last 25 years who have given me the opportunity to walk this creative path I call my life. They have consistently challenged me to continue learning, growing, and sharing.

CONTENTS

INTRODUCTION

WE'VE ALL READ ABOUT the legendary inventors, scientists, and designers whose discoveries changed the world forever. And the way the stories go, many of their brilliant insights seemed like destiny: James Watt got the idea for the steam engine from watching his mother's tea kettle boil on the stove; Alexander Fleming discovered penicillin when a petri dish was accidentally left open all night; and we all remember the legend about Sir Isaac Newton and the apple.

Whatever actually led to each of those defining moments, for centuries we have made certain assumptions about the men and women whose ingenuity still inspires us today. Although their biographies reveal admirable work ethic and perseverance, we presumed that they were also born with a unique set of gifts that enabled them to see ordinary things in a different light. This kind of genius, we were told, was given to a select few. You either had it or you didn't.

For a very long time, this conventional wisdom went unchallenged. Standardized tests given in elementary school were used to divide children into different ability groups, often for their entire academic careers. If no one had recognized creative genius in us by high school, we assumed we didn't have it. Once we entered a career track, we were encouraged to work hard and pay our dues, and then success—at whatever level we were destined for—would come.

But what if that's not how genius works? What if Einstein and Edison were simply using their brains in a different way than how we are using ours? Ralph Waldo Emerson once made this observation about the creative process: "Bare lists of words are found suggestive to an imaginative and excited mind." This implies that creativity is a state of mind rather than an innate ability. What if ingenuity isn't *given*, as much as it must be *awakened*?

For 25 years, I have coached executives and other corporate leaders—both in Europe and the United States—who sought a greater measure of success. Many of these men and women had already accomplished more than most professionals would hope to achieve in a lifetime, but they were looking for ways to take their companies and their personal performances to the next level. To make this kind of change, I had to help them access deeper levels of creativity, ingenuity, and innovation. This potential had always been inside them; they simply needed to learn to release it more effectively.

In addition to more than a decade of experience as a corporate executive and my subsequent education in psychology and human behavioral sciences, my years of work as an executive coach have motivated me to become a lifelong student of the human mind. I constantly research new coaching techniques, as well as develop new creativity models to help my clients reach their potential. Throughout the years I have kept the methods and models that yield the greatest results and discarded the rest.

Time after time, I have been astounded by what happens when you teach an individual to access even just a little more of his or her creative potential. I have watched client companies increase their revenues by billions of dollars. I have seen the leaders who apply my techniques reduce their turnover of valued talent, reduce their costs, and optimize their productivity. They have also been able to accelerate their pace of innovation and design, and launch new products and brands, while many have also opened new business locations around the globe. But perhaps even more importantly, the theories and techniques outlined in this book have helped my clients—some of the busiest people in the world who are under tremendous pressure—enjoy their lives more, both at work and at home.

Not every idea or method in this book will appeal to you, but some of them undoubtedly will. Give them a try. I guarantee if you apply them consistently, you will see results. Let me know how it goes; I would love to hear about your experiences. You can easily find me at: scott.cochrane@theboldmindgroup.com.

One

Time to Let Go of New Habits

IN 1971, TWO BROTHERS opened an 800-square-foot used bookstore in my hometown of Ann Arbor, Michigan. Throughout the next two decades, this family-run enterprise would grow into Borders Books, the giant chain with more than 650 stores and thousands of employees. Borders created an amazing in-store experience, bringing the joy of browsing through thousands of titles to areas of the country that had never had bookstores before. Two years after its IPO in 1995, Borders stock hit an all-time high. Yet just 16 years later, the company that one publisher had called "the envy of the industry" filed for bankruptcy. What happened?

There are many reasons that businesses close their doors. We've all heard the dismal statistics about how often new businesses fail. The precise numbers are hotly disputed, typically ranging from a grim nine out of 10 to a more optimistic five out of 10 enterprises shutting down within the first year to 18 months. Writing in *Forbes*, Eric T. Wagner offered five reasons for such failures: lack of connection with customers, lack of a unique value proposition, lack of effective marketing, lack of effective leadership, and lack of a profitable business model.[1] And certainly if your organization is lacking any of these vital components, it will not be around for long.

But what about the companies that have all these ingredients and do rise to great success—as Borders did—and then suddenly and unexpectedly disappear? These fail for multiple reasons, including poor financial leadership and bad marketing decisions. Sometimes a dramatic shift in consumer behavior proves too much for a company to overcome. The A&P grocery store chain—founded in 1859 and so dominant in the 1940s that some considered it a monopoly—recently filed for bankruptcy. In truth, the company never recovered from the population shift of families from urban centers to the burgeoning suburbs during the 1970s. Grocery shoppers were no longer walking to neighborhood stores in central cities;

instead they were driving to larger grocery stores with huge parking lots and lower prices. A&P lost millions of dollars as a result.

Often, however, it is a new technology or a new way of thinking about an existing product that interferes with the business model of a strong, well-run company. Disruptive technologies are really nothing new, although the term has only recently become popular. Wagon-wheel makers lost their livelihood to automobiles, and cowboys were no longer needed to herd cattle over hundreds of miles once railroads could carry refrigerated cars full of beef.

In Borders' case, the disruptive technology was two-fold: deeply discounted online books sales and e-books. The company was clearly aware of these threats, but their strategic responses proved either poorly calculated or extraordinarily unlucky. Faced with two such fundamental challenges to its business model—which relied on in-store purchases of paper books—Borders continued to expand its number of retail stores. This was a very risky move, involving immense expenditures in real estate, construction, and ongoing overhead.

Borders' decision seems foolhardy in hindsight, but its leaders correctly understood that part of its appeal was the in-store experience. They hoped that by opening new locations that experience would continue to translate into profits. Borders succeeded in reaching new markets, but its customers began browsing books in the store and then buying them later online; in the meantime the company accrued hundreds of millions of dollars of real estate debt.

Building more stores was not Borders' only misstep. It started carrying large inventories of CDs and DVDs just before digital music and media cut deeply into the profitability of both. It hired Amazon to handle its online marketing and e-books, and of course Amazon later rose to become one of the online competitors that put Borders out of business.

It is easy to forget that Borders was a disruptive innovator at its inception. It was a big box store, undercutting prices and putting many small independent bookstores out of business. One of its founders developed a software program that revolutionized the way bookstores managed inventory and projected sales. Yet like too many large, successful companies, its leaders were not able to react quickly enough to the rapid changes in the market. Barnes and Noble, by contrast, survives with its own extensive online offerings and the Nook, its own e-book reader.

Accelerating Change

Borders was a well-run company that offered products and an experience that all of its customers loved. For two decades it had a competitive advantage in its inventory software, but when the digital revolution hit, it simply couldn't make the necessary adjustments quickly enough.

Kodak—a company that was extremely profitable for more than a hundred years—encountered the same problem with digital photography. If Kodak had been in the business of selling cameras, it could have made the transition smoothly. It easily could have sold digital cameras since a Kodak engineer had invented the first one. But Kodak's business model relied on selling cameras at razor-thin margins, making the bulk of its profit on film. Despite being aware of the approaching digital revolution for decades, it did not adjust its business model quickly enough to survive. Fujifilm's leaders, on the other hand, understood the changes on the horizon, made drastic cuts, and acquired multiple digital startups, which helped them weather the storm successfully.

As with Borders, it is easy to criticize Kodak's leaders in hindsight. Yet it is not hard to see how a company that had been so successful for so long could have difficulty grasping the impending death of their business model. What truly innovative leaders must understand is that death, without fail, comes for us all.

In Greek mythology, Thanatos was the personification of death. Unlike the dreaded Hades—terrifying god of the underworld—Thanatos was not traditionally feared. He was believed to carry people off gently when the fates had decreed that their time had come. No business idea, no technology, no innovation, no product, or service has eternal life. Part of unleashing our true creative potential is understanding that everything we create will endure for a finite amount of time, and then Thanatos—in the form of an e-book, a digital camera, or whatever new idea is currently changing the world—will come to carry it off. This is not an event to be feared; it is to be expected and prepared for.

Expecting change does not necessarily make it feel less disruptive. At the turn of the 20th century, parents worried when mail began to be delivered to computers instead of to the post office. For the first time, young ladies could get letters from young men without their parents' knowledge. Today, parents can barely keep up with the video- and photo-sharing technologies that allow their children to stay in touch with friends 24 hours a day.

Furthermore, technological change is accelerating. Thomas Edison invented the phonograph in 1877. The vinyl record appeared in 1948, the cassette tape in 1963, the compact disc in 1982. When the first iPod appeared in 2001, people no longer had to purchase physical objects in order to buy music. Instead, they paid to download it off the web, and profit margins soared. Just seven years later, Spotify launched its digital streaming service. This allowed customers to pay a set fee (or no fee at all if they didn't mind a few ads) to listen to unlimited selections, disrupting the business model of paying for individual downloads.

Staying Flexible

As we age, our joints and muscles tend to become stiff. If we do not take the time to exercise and stretch, we will lose flexibility and may eventually lose our mobility altogether. The same process can occur with our minds. After performing tasks a certain way for so many years, the idea of changing or adapting seems infinitely more daunting than it did when we were in our teens.

Cognitive rigidity—the inability to consider different viewpoints or innovative solutions to a problem—afflicts all of us at times to varying degrees. At its mildest, it is merely the inability to change one's opinion about a subject, even when presented with significant evidence to the contrary. At its most extreme, it can involve a nearly sociopathic lack of empathy for others. Ironically the more expertise we develop in a particular field, the more difficult it can be for us to look at things in new or different ways. Some have described this phenomenon as the "tyranny of experience." We become captive to what we know, sometimes at the expense of learning something new.

Cognitive rigidity is a common symptom in children with Asperger's syndrome and high-functioning autism, causing them to have tremendous difficulty coping with changes in the rules or routine they are expected to follow, as well as with making transitions from one environment to the next. Many neurologists believe this is because the part of the brain that controls executive function—impulse control, mental flexibility, and planning—are not working properly. In a much less extreme way, adults can experience similar problems if they do not "stretch" or challenge their brains to remain sufficiently flexible. Entire organizations become accustomed to a certain set of "rules" governing the market and to a certain business model. They become deeply uncomfortable with any idea or proposal that deviates from that set of assumptions.

It seems likely that this kind of rigid thinking was part of Kodak's problem. As Avi Dan wrote in *Forbes*, "Immensely successful companies can become myopic . . . Kodak's story of failing has its roots in its success, which made it resistant to change. Its insular corporate culture believed that its strength was in its brand and marketing, and it underestimated the threat of digital."[2]

Corporations are not the only ones that suffer from this problem. During World War II, the Americans broke the Japanese diplomatic code in 1940, yet Japanese advisers continually assured their leaders that such a feat was not humanly possible. This allowed the Americans to know precisely where every Japanese supply ship was stationed and attack them with submarines. In 1943, they were able to kill one of their most effective leaders, Admiral Yamamoto, when his flying schedule was put on the air.

Tension and Balance in the Creative Process

So how do we avoid rigid thinking? Obviously we cannot reject all routine and refuse to develop specialized expertise. In fact, human beings need habits and routines to survive. All kinds of necessary activities—brushing our teeth, tying our shoes, or working out for an hour at the gym—need to be performed over and over. And the more often we repeat an action or a set of actions, the less mental energy we have to exert to perform them. *New York Times* business writer Charles Duhigg explained in his book *The Power of Habit* that habits are a three-part process: the trigger, the behavior itself, and the reward. Whether the habit is good, bad, or neutral is immaterial. The smell of a donut can catch our attention (trigger), we purchase and eat the donut (behavior), and experience delicious taste and a sugar high (reward). Once this process is repeated often enough, the brain automates it, and we no longer have to think about what we're doing.

Habits are vital to conserve our mental energy for more important tasks. Habitual behaviors allow us to do two things at once, such as drive to work while carrying on a conversation, or listen to music while exercising or cooking dinner. Organizations also need routines. A salesperson who comes up with a different way to ask for certain pieces of information each time he or she speaks to a prospect will waste valuable time and energy (and lose valuable information) when compared to the person who works from a script that is market tested and requests all the needed data. If accountants have to rediscover every month how to process invoices, it will take much longer than if they have a set system to deal with them.

But habits have a dark side too. It is possible to become so automated that we lose the ability to function outside our daily routines, leading to dangerous levels of rigidity in the way we think. Sometimes—as ironic as it seems—the creative process can become routine: an exercise in going through the motions rather than creating something new.

Throughout history, various cultures have coped differently with the inherent tension between the need for routine and the desire of spontaneity and flexibility. In his book *The Teachings of Don Juan: The Yaqui Way of Knowledge,* anthropologist Carlos Castaneda explores Yaqui Indian shamanism in central Mexico. The Yaqui think of themselves as warriors in a dangerous world, and as a result resist developing routines and patterns in their lives that they believe will make them vulnerable. For example, they point out the danger of walking on the same road every day, noting that such a practice makes one susceptible to assault.[3] Although numerous scholars have disputed the academic validity of his findings, Castaneda's descriptions paint a compelling picture of how easy it is to "get into a rut" in our daily routines, and how difficult it can be to break out.

The Problem with Brainstorming

For decades most of the West has approached the creative process with variations on the "brainstorming model," made popular in the 1950s. Yet for years I have coached my clients to apply entirely different techniques. Once I helped a company to re-brand a soft drink that had been losing market share for years. I set before a group of several of their leaders a plethora of items: an umbrella, a rubber tube, a coffee grinder, a toaster, and a vase, and then I asked them to choose one. After considering their choices, they selected the coffee grinder. We proceeded to identify and then apply specific characteristics of the coffee grinder to the soft drink branding issue as a creativity exercise. (I share more on this creativity technique in Chapter 7.) By the end of the session, they had come up with an entirely fresh message about the beverage, which launched a successful marketing campaign and revitalized sales for the first time in years.

Why did this approach work? For decades, scientists assumed that the adult brain was like a vault of information. You could make deposits and withdrawals, but you couldn't really change its structure or design. We knew our brains could be injured by trauma, of course, but we really didn't think they could be improved much, other than by cramming them full of more data.

This understanding of the brain shaped the way we understood the creative process. Brainstorming seemed to harness perfectly the potential of a group of people. Get all those information vaults together in a boardroom and have everyone dump their contents onto the table. Then everyone would be able to examine the information supplied by everyone else in the room, and the best ideas would rise to the top.

Most of us are familiar with the "ground rules" of a classic brainstorming session. There is no such thing as a "stupid" idea: no judgment or criticism is permitted. Furthermore, the wackier the idea the better; everyone is encouraged to think outside the box. All participants are expected to contribute as many ideas as they can, and whenever possible, ideas should be combined or build off of one another. These, we were told, were the key ingredients to release originality and innovation.

In one sense, it is easy to understand why brainstorming became popular with corporate executives: you get to hear from everyone, and everyone feels heard. But more often than we care to admit, brainstorming proves far better at producing quantity than quality. If we are honest, brainstorming sessions frequently yield a mass of mediocre ideas rather than a few brilliant ones.

There are several reasons for this: First, the group environment of brainstorming sessions naturally biases the entire operation toward the more extroverted members. Yet the world is full of brilliant problem-solvers who are not naturally comfortable sharing their ideas in a group setting; you will rarely hear from them in a brainstorming session. Dominant personalities—rather than better ideas—tend to carry the day. If an authority figure is present in the session, most individuals will watch his or her response for cues to determine what their own should be. In short, unintentional groupthink becomes a powerful current, steering the discussion in the direction of convention and drowning out originality and innovation.

That's a great collection of the best ideas we had before starting this meeting...

The combination of the soft drink with the coffee grinder forced the small group I was working with to form drastically new associations rather than follow the loudest voice. This awakened a different part of their brains, and that is what ultimately allowed them to come up with a marketing campaign that was authentically new and different.

Unleashing a New Creative Power

"Creativity is a shapechanger," Dr. Clarissa Pinkola Estés tells us in her best-selling classic, *Women Who Run with the Wolves*. She describes creative energy as a rushing river, surging and overwhelming everything in its path. She goes on to explain:

> If we are gasping for creative energy; if we have trouble pulling down the fertile, if we have difficulty focusing on our personal vision, acting on it or following through with it, then something has gone wrong at the water spill juncture between the headwaters and the tributary. Or the creative waters are flowing through a polluted environment wherein the life forms or imagination are killed off before they can grow to maturity.[4]

According to Dr. Estes, creativity is not something we have to find; it is something we must cease impeding or poisoning. Once we stop blocking the creative force, we can expect to be overwhelmed by it. But what are the barriers that we erect against creativity? In my years of coaching and consulting, I have observed several.

- *Inflexibility*: As we've already touched on, rigid thinking can be a powerful barrier against innovation. Kodak's leaders simply could not envision a world in which their brand recognition and business model were not enough to carry the day. They could not see the bold new world unfolding before them until it was far too late.

- *Control*: People with controlling person-alities often rise to leadership positions because of their diligence and aggressive-ness. And in many cases such leaders have some important qualities: they can be decisive, goal-oriented and quick-thinking. Unfortunately, they can also be impatient, judgmental, and distrusting of ideas that are not theirs, and those characteristics quench creativity.

  Just a few years after inventing the smartphone, Blackberry found itself out-flanked by Apple and Android. According to the investigative report *Inside the Fall of BlackBerry: How the Smartphone Inventor Failed to Adapt*, "RIM [Research in Motion, later known as BlackBerry] exerted tight control over developers before it would sign off on their apps for use on BlackBerrys, stifling creativity." According to Trevor Nimegeers, an entrepreneur whose company was hired to develop apps for Blackberry, app developers didn't like working under such tightly controlled conditions, preferring to do business with the more flexible leaders of companies like Instagram and Tumblr.[5]

- *Fear*: Fear is an understandable response to any change that seems to upset our business model, but it will also reliably stifle any creative impulses in an instant. In fact, the chemical response of our brains to fear prepares us to fight, not create. (More on this later in the book!) Fear doesn't have to be provoked by a new technology, market shift, or competitor. Sometimes it is provoked by a colleague or leader to whom we compare ourselves or our accomplishments. As Dr. Estés writes, "Perhaps one so admires the gifts of another, and/or the seeming benefits earned or received by another, that one becomes expert in mimicry, sadly content to be a mediocre 'them,' rather than developing one's own unique gifts to their absolute and startling depths."[6]

- *Egotism*: Egotism is not the same as confidence. In fact, egotistical behavior typically masks deep insecurities about one's own worth or capabilities. Egotistical leaders are easily offended and deeply concerned with who gets credit for a new idea or project. At the same time, they are often very eager to absolve themselves of blame when something goes wrong rather than find a solution. The ego devotes more energy to defending old turf in a company than to creating something new. Perhaps worst of all, egotistical leaders have such a distorted view of themselves that they struggle to evaluate anything objectively, including ideas. The sense of entitlement to success that accompanies egotism blocks the flow of creative energy. Egotistical leaders refuse to question themselves and hate to be questioned by others.

For millennia, seekers and shamans have sought to break down these barriers to creativity by taking hallucinogenic drugs or working themselves into a state of euphoria. But such holy men also have important rituals, kept hundreds or even thousands of years. In the chapters that follow, we will examine what this delicate and dynamic balance looks like for the modern company.

Conclusion

When we look at successful companies competing in various markets today, we see three basic kinds of activity: 1) companies that work to preserve what they have, even in the face of tremendous change; 2) those that react to changes effectively; and 3) those that are creating the change itself.

And of course just because a company is creating the change today does not mean it will not be forced to react to change created by someone else tomorrow.

Monday morning quarterbacking is infinitely easier than solidifying the game plan on Saturday night. At the end of the day, it is impossible to know precisely why Kodak, Borders, and BlackBerry failed to react and innovate the way that Fujifilm, Barnes and Noble, and Android did. But we can look at some of the characteristics they had in common and learn from them.

- *They were all disrupted instead of causing the disruption.* All three companies had their tried and true business models upended by new technologies. Kodak, despite spending millions on research and development and inventing the digital camera, still failed to cope with the digital revolution. Kodak's engineers were innovating, but Kodak's leadership was not.
- *They didn't react to the disruption quickly enough.* By the time these companies were

fully aware of what was going on and its implications for their market, they were too burdened by debt or investment in the wrong direction to dig themselves out. Disruptive change requires both accurate understanding and quick, decisive actions in response.

- *They would not accept the death of their business model.* Thanatos comes for us all, and all the denial and resistance in the world will not change that. Kodak refused to realize that their days of making money from the printing of photographs were over, Borders failed to adjust to the reality of e-commerce and digital music, and BlackBerry couldn't accept the supreme importance of apps to smartphone users. The rest is history.

- *Their confidence appeared to be misplaced.* Successful companies are always at risk of becoming complacent and resting on their laurels. Not every innovator is personally humble, but all companies that consistently innovate recognize that no one holds a monopoly on creativity. They anticipate the market, listen to its signals, and try new things.

It can be incredibly easy for company leaders to surround themselves with people who tell them what they want to hear instead of challenging their assumptions and warning them about disruptive change. Sometimes the corporate structure itself discourages creativity, preventing companies from moving forward. Sometimes routine invades the very creative process, producing warmed leftovers instead of exciting new possibilities.

Any company can be derailed by disruptive technology or marketing, but not every company is positioning itself to be the source of that disruptive change. In the next chapter, we will examine what it takes to do that.

Two

The Bold New World

THE AVERAGE AMERICAN HOUSEHOLD today contains countless examples of technology that would have been almost inconceivable 50 years ago. Labor-saving devices, communication, and entertainment are literally at our fingertips 24 hours a day. The way we buy, sell, work, and even socialize has been transformed by innovative individuals and companies that have brought us products and services we never knew we needed but now can't live without.

There are many different ways to innovate. Not every successful company will invent an iPad or start Amazon. Some will simply develop an app for the iPad or use Amazon to sell vintage clothing or designer dog collars. In fact, not every successful innovation has to be trendy or cool. And although it feels sometimes as if innovation is driven almost entirely by technological advancements, this is not necessarily the case either.

But there are some qualities and conditions that are necessary—or at least extremely helpful—for innovation to take place. In this chapter we'll examine the companies that are creating the bold new world we live in and the lessons we can learn from them. We'll look for those components that are vital to innovation so we can implement them in our own businesses.

Creativity and Innovation

Creativity and innovation are often used interchangeably, but they are not quite the same thing. Creativity can be defined many different ways, but for our purposes we can think of it as the ability to come up with a truly new or original idea. Innovation, in the business world, is the application of creativity in any number of ways, some of which hopefully turn out to be profitable. Here is the catch: not all creativity will lead to innovation, and not all innovation will lead to something profitable. Anyone who offers you a formula to come up with new ideas that always translate into profitable innovations is selling you snake oil.

When we think of business innovation changing the world, it is very easy to think solely in terms of new technology. But in reality there are many different kinds of innovation.

- *Innovative product*: For centuries, countless creative individuals have offered us new products that seemed previously unimaginable. Whether it was a telephone, a lawnmower, a smoke detector, or an iPad, new inventions continue to create new markets for themselves.

- *Innovative service:* A service innovation often, but not always, follows a cultural or technological change. For example, the application of dental materials to fingernails led to the development of artificial nails and the eventual explosion of businesses offering manicures and pedicures. When more women began working outside the home, the number of businesses offering services that stay-at-home mothers and wives often did—from meal preparation to dog-walking—likewise increased in number.

- *Innovative improvement:* The old axiom about building a better mousetrap still holds true today. If you can develop a new version of an existing product that works significantly better, the world will beat a path to your door. James Dyson did not invent the vacuum cleaner, but he developed a vacuum that used centripetal separators instead of the centrifugal fan used in traditional vacuum cleaners. Its superior performance launched his company and sparked countless imitators.

Service delivery can be improved as well. Accenture innovated the way that consultants work by reimagining their offices. Recognizing that its consultants spent the majority of their time out of the office and with clients, they were one of the first major firms to implement "hot desking." This innovative office layout enabled them to save on overhead costs, expand their operations more quickly, and allowed employees to come and go as needed.

- *Production innovation:* Sometimes a creative new way to create or assemble a product will greatly reduce the time or cost of production. Before Henry Ford produced automobiles with an assembly line and standardized parts, only the very wealthy could afford them. Ford made the Model T the car that everyone could afford.

  Of course cost-cutting isn't the only reason to innovate production. During World War II, American shipbuilders were able to reduce the time it took to produce a new naval ship from 196 days to just 27 days. They produced more than a thousand in just a few years, greatly aiding the Allies' ability to win the war.[1]

- *Supply chain/delivery innovation:* A century ago, Sears and Montgomery Ward brought factory-made dishes and other household products through mail-order catalogues to millions of Americans living in rural communities. They were not inventing anything new; they just came up with a new way of delivering the products to customers more easily. Today, millions of internet-based companies are doing exactly the same thing.

- *Marketing innovation:* Sometimes a creative change in the way a product is marketed to the consumer can revolutionize a company or an industry. When the FDA allowed prune growers to begin labeling their products as "dried plums" (which is what they are), sales—which had been in steady decline for some time—increased 5.5 percent in the first year. In a sense, any kind of style or trend-oriented industry (fashion, in particular) can be seen as driven by marketing innovations.

- *Business model innovation:* Business model innovations involve changes in the source of profitability for a company. Uber provides essentially the same service as a traditional taxi company, but its business model does not involve owning or maintaining any cars. The consumer experience is not very different, but the innovation was made possible by a technological development (ubiquitous smartphones and a new app). As discussed in Chapter 1, the digital camera had no effect on Kodak's hold on the camera market, but it devastated its business model, which relied on selling film for the bulk of its profits.

- *Experiential innovation:* Sometimes it is not the product or service that changes, but the way the customer experiences the product or service. Starbucks created high-quality coffee and also a chain of stores that offered customers a place to gather and chat. Many bookstores offer story time for preschool-aged children so stay-at-home parents and nannies have somewhere to take them during the day. Restaurants may innovate by experimenting with open mic nights or other live entertainment rather than changing their menu or pricing. Some health clubs feature a luxury experience, some an intense competitive workout environment, and others offer a chance for singles to meet and mingle, while the overall service the customer is paying for remains the same.

From the Garage to Google

When scientists look for life on other planets, they know ahead of time what conditions are necessary to support it. The proper distance from a star, a protective atmosphere, and the presence of water are all crucial ingredients for life to flourish. It is not too different with creativity. We can look at companies—big and small—and learn a lot about the environmental ingredients that encourage creativity and innovation to flourish.

Innovation is not defined by scale. A child laying out all her outfits for the week on Sunday evening is innovating the way she prepares for school, saving herself a few minutes every morning. A multibillion-dollar company that tweaks its manufacturing process may save millions in production costs each year. Yet, the creative processes that give rise to these two innovations are not very different.

Do giant companies possess a significant innovative advantage over one or two entrepreneurs working out of a home office or a garage? Ready cash can be important in order to experiment, produce prototypes, and to launch products, but it is not a necessary precondition for innovative ideas. In fact, as we discussed in the last chapter, plenty of huge companies with vast resources fail to innovate at all or cease to innovate effectively. So what do large and small innovators have in common?

Among large innovators, Apple is perhaps most famous for bringing us what we want before we know we want it. The brainchild of the late Steve Jobs does not necessarily *invent* new technology, but they innovate by focusing on how people use and *interact with* technology. They also create sleek, attractive, high-quality products that set trends and end up in the hands of celebrities and teenagers alike.

Of course no one can talk about large innovators without mentioning Google, the company that perennially tops multiple lists of the most innovative companies. Reams have been written about this amazing organization and everything they do to ensure that they never lose their creative edge. Google is known to invest millions into research and development (R&D), but this alone does not guarantee innovation. After all, Kodak also invested heavily into R&D but was unable to capitalize on the results.

So what makes Google so enviable in the bold new world? Here are a few more of its well-established practices that seem to keep the new ideas coming.

- Google leaders make it clear that they do not believe they have a monopoly on creativity. They look for ideas everywhere and are constantly forming partnerships and acquiring startups. By using Linux, a free and open source operating system, Google allows its users to innovate for them and with them.

- Google builds creativity into their employees' schedules. For years, the company has encouraged employees to take 20 percent of their time and devote it to a project that they are passionate about.

- Google does not stigmatize failure. As their chief social evangelist Gopi Kallayil told *Fast Company*, "Failure is the way to be innovative and successful. You can fail with pride."[2]

- Google does not wait for everything to be perfect before launching something new; their mindset is "ship and iterate" by releasing new products often and allowing users to point out flaws and potential improvements.[3]

- Google does not worry about making an innovative idea profitable right away. They believe profitability will follow if they focus sufficiently on the user/customer.[4]

- Google takes its mission statement (to organize the world's information and make it universally accessible and useful) very seriously. There is plenty of evidence that suggests that human beings are much more creative when they are motivated by a sense of purpose that is larger than themselves.

Now let's consider a couple of well-known startup innovators. YouTube founders Chad Hurley, Steve

Chen, and Jawed Karim got the idea for the site in 2004. Karim told *USA Today* that he first thought of creating a video sharing site when Janet Jackson's famous wardrobe malfunction at that year's Super Bowl half-time show and the Indian Ocean earthquake (and subsequent tsunami) prompted millions to go online searching for videos of both events. The three men, all former employees of PayPal, discussed the possibility of starting a site at which such sought-after videos could be easily uploaded and viewed.

In April 2005, the trio uploaded the first video to YouTube. In October 2006, Google bought them out for 1.7 billion dollars in stock. As of this writing, YouTube videos receive several billion views each day, launching the careers of countless musicians, athletes, and entertainers.

Instagram founders Kevin Systrom and Mike Krieger both got their feet wet in established technology-oriented companies such as Meebo (an instant messaging company), Google, and Twitter. They studied every photo-sharing application they could find and decided to develop an app that combined the popular filters available on other photo-sharing sites with a social component modeled after Facebook. They tested and refined their idea until it became easy to use and launched it in October of 2010, just as the iPhone 4 was being released with its improved digital camera. Instagram got 25,000 users the first day and a million in the first month. In April 2012, Systrom and Krieger sold their startup to Facebook for 1 billion dollars, 300 million in cash, and the rest in Facebook stock. Their company employed just 13 people at the time.

So what are the takeaways from these wildly successful innovators? The first is obvious, but worth exploring for a moment. Whether it occurs in a huge company like Google or in a tiny company like Instagram, creativity—and the innovation that comes from it—is a product of a human brain (or two or three brains working together). You will notice that Google does not gather its employees in groups of a thousand or a hundred to maximize their creativity. Rather, they allow them to spend a certain percentage of their time alone or in small groups in order to foster the creative spirit.

This is not to say that larger groups cannot come up with creative ideas, especially with the right coaching. However, it should be noted that large size and scale are not necessary to the creative process. Furthermore, as we saw in the last chapter, the routine and subsequent rigidity associated with a larger company often hinders the creative process. While thousands of companies are working to mimic Google, Google is working constantly to retain the freshness and flexibility that comes with being a tiny startup.

We can also see that creative inspiration does not follow a set pattern. The idea for YouTube was sparked suddenly by outside events, while Instagram's concept seemed to develop more gradually as Systrom and Krieger tested and scrapped various apps. Google works to provide an environment where both of these kinds of processes can unfold at their own pace.

We can also note that motivation and purpose serve as important ingredients in the creative process. The founders of both YouTube and Instagram had previously worked for other companies before and were deeply motivated to do something on their own. Google works to ensure all employees share the company's mission and vision, even though they come from all over the world and from many different walks of life.

There is no question that the possibility of making large profits motivates people to think creatively. And it is certainly easier for a large company with loads of cash not to worry about money in the short term and invest in long-term potential. However, there is something about the future-oriented mindset that focuses on what is possible that seems almost indispensable to authentic innovation. It is an organic process that can be encouraged but not tightly controlled, and the leaders of innovative companies understand that.

The Right Kind of Collaboration

As companies like Google repeatedly demonstrate, the right kind of collaboration can spark tremendous creativity and subsequent innovation. But what does this look like for organizations that don't possess Google or Apple's inherent attractiveness to potential collaborators? That answer is often just a matter of looking at what is around us with the right set of eyes.

Not long ago, I was speaking to a director at a business school where I serve as a senior adviser to the Dean. She was deeply frustrated with the fundraising goal they had been given by their parent university and felt she had no support to help her with the enormous task before her. She also complained that she had professors with PhDs helping her put together binders full of information for the events she was coordinating because she was so short staffed.

I asked her three questions: 1) How many local businesses were "partners" with the business school? 2) How many graduate students did they have? 3) How could new technologies potentially reduce the need for binders and physical material? She answered my questions, and I saw the wheels begin to turn. I proposed that I would coordinate a mastermind speaker series with other local business leaders that would serve as an ongoing fundraiser for the business school's responsibility toward the university's endowment. At my suggestion, she also began a volunteer program for graduate students who wanted more business experience and a chance to interact with some of the leaders who would be speaking. She also contacted the technology department at the university to explore different alternatives to physical binders. By simply looking around her with a different set of eyes, she began three collaborative efforts that were extremely beneficial to all parties involved.

Innovation of Identity

"Rebranding" has become a vastly overused term these days, but sometimes an innovative identity change is necessary for a company's survival. The bold new world can become a hostile place for some well-established organizations, and it is important to do something bold to keep up. Just as with any type of innovation, not every new identity will be a home run. But in some industries, sticking with the status quo is simply slow suicide.

Sometimes the reinvention is a true death and resurrection experience. Thanatos does not just come for a particular product or profit model; he comes for the entire company. So it was with Nokia, a Finnish company that began in 1865 as a lumber business. In the early 1900s it expanded into rubber and cable and then emerged as a global leader in communications in the 1990s. The list continues: cosmetics giant Avon started as a door-to-door book-seller, Scotch tape manufacturer 3M was a mining company, and toymaker Hasbro began as a seller of textile remnants.

But not every successful reinvention has to be quite that dramatic. A few decades ago, there were more than 300 department stores in the United States, and most were doing a brisk business. The overwhelming majority of purchases were made at physical stores, and indoor malls were a destination for adults and teens alike. Today, those same malls are closing regularly and many of their former anchor stores—Sears and J.C. Penney to name a couple—are struggling as well.

Many analysts have blamed the economic downturn along with internet purchasing for the death of the enclosed mall, but that does not tell the entire story. Outdoor town centers—modeled after urban downtown strips—are popping up everywhere, and the store that has reinvented itself successfully to keep pace is Target. Dayton Hudson—Target's parent company—actually began as a dry goods company in 1902 and grew into a chain of department stores. Dayton Hudson opened its first Target store in 1962; as department stores began to struggle, Target became the company's largest source of revenue. Today, Target is the second largest discount retailer in the United States, behind Walmart.

But what about businesses that don't span the entire country, holding massive assets and cash reserves? Can they successfully reinvent themselves as well? Silver Diner is a regional restaurant chain based in Rockville, Maryland. It began in 1989 as a nostalgia-themed diner with jukeboxes in each booth that played classic rock and a menu filled with American comfort food. Founders Robert Giaimo and Chef Ype Von Hengst wanted to build a restaurant at which families could bring their children and seniors could remember earlier, simpler times.

During the 1990s, the chain opened several locations in Maryland, Virginia, and New Jersey. In 1996, they received investment to go public and expand, trading on the Nasdaq. Its stock price peaked that year at eight dollars a share, but by 2002 was trading at just 19 cents. Silver Diner went private again and decided to reevaluate everything.

The owners began their makeover by voluntarily getting rid of trans fats in their cooking and putting nutritional information on their menu. As the decade wore on and the economy tightened, nearly all restaurants saw their earnings drop. Most were working to cut costs by cutting labor or offering smaller portions and fewer menu options in order to survive. Silver Diner made a bold choice; they decided to reimagine the diner experience for the next generation. They overhauled the menu, completely reinventing themselves as a farm-to-table restaurant by buying locally. They featured hormone- and antibiotic-free meat and dairy, and offered options for vegetarian, vegan, and gluten-free customers. But they also kept the nostalgic décor and the affordable prices to keep their older customers happy. The kids' menus featured healthy sides and drinks (although fries and soda were still available upon request) and it earned particular praise from nutritionists and parents, who were thrilled to see their offspring eating salmon and fruit.

Today, if you visit one of Silver Diner's 15 mid-Atlantic locations, you will see crowds of all ages. They boast the largest chain of diners in the country, with the highest average sales per store if its kind. In an era when many other larger restaurant chains are closing locations, Silver Diner continues to thrive.

Bring Value First

Google does not worry about making an innovation profitable right away. YouTube's required bandwidth costs millions each month, leading many to speculate that its expenses initially outpaced its advertising revenues. Everyone knows Amazon lost money for the first nine years it was in business, and other successful companies like Tesla and FedEx took a while to turn a profit as well.

Of course, smaller companies without a patient venture capitalist may not be able to dump a lot of cash into an idea for years before it begins to show a return. But what can they take from these examples? The problem isn't thinking about money, because making money is always an important end goal. After all, if an innovation doesn't make money eventually, it most likely is not meeting a real need.

The reason we don't want to focus on money in the short term is that there will always be shortsighted things we can do to generate immediate cash that can prove fatal to innovation in the long run. How many times do we hear about a new CEO taking charge of a company, cutting staff, and posting a huge improvement in quarterly profits, only to see the entire operation fall apart a year or two later?

The bold new world is created by companies that can see beyond short-term cash issues to what will bring true value to customers in the long haul. Perhaps some of the most dramatic examples occur in emerging markets. For example, innovation in mobile banking took place in developing countries—where most banks weren't interested in doing business—long before it hit the rest of the world. The general lack of brick-and-mortar banks led countries like India to skip directly to wireless banking. M-Pesa, a cellphone-based money transfer and microfinancing service, was launched in 2007 in Kenya and Tanzania.

Not every emerging market innovation has been supremely high tech either. China's runaway investment in African countries has mostly involved straightforward trade—usually finished Chinese goods for African raw materials. For decades most western countries viewed African nations as recipients of foreign aid, as opposed to an emerging consumer market or a trade partner. Trade between China and Africa was just 10 billion dollars in 2000; in 2013 it topped 200 billion in commodities ranging from food to minerals and oil. This exchange has led to an explosion of roads, airports, and other vital components of infrastructure that will enable African commerce to continue to expand. Such investments are long-term—it is hard to see an ROI on a major highway in the first several months or years—but they hold unimaginable potential for the future.

Naturally, the Chinese government's investment in Africa is full of controversy, from its effect on the environment to other ethical and cultural concerns. Yet with Africa housing nearly 12 million square miles of land, much of it still unused and full of natural resources, China will undoubtedly have an important seat at the table as that untapped potential is realized to a greater degree. And the fact remains that both sides of the partnership are seeing tangible benefits as well.

Conclusion

So who is creating the bold new world? Companies that are not afraid to let go of the old and embrace something entirely different and new. Leaders who are open to ideas from anywhere and everywhere, and whose openness makes others want to share with them. Such leaders form effective alliances and partnerships with others that prove mutually beneficial. They see potential where others don't, and they are willing to take risks others aren't.

Industry-rocking innovations are brought to market by people who are willing to release something before it is perfect and fix it as they go. Perhaps more than anything else, we see that creativity does not arise from a particular formula or a step-by-step process that is precisely duplicable, but rather from an environment that is supportive and flexible enough to encourage everything to come together.

Three

Creative Power and the Power of Creation

DID YOU EVER DREAM up a crazy idea as a child, such as a tiny rocket ship that would take you to the moon or a castle filled with dozens of hidden passageways? Most of us had all kinds of wild ideas when we were young; perhaps we drew pictures or wrote stories about them. Yet, as with most of our ideas, they never moved beyond the conceptual stage to become reality.

Creativity can sound like an intimidating concept, but it is really no more than the state of imagination that almost all of us experienced as children. So why do we often feel a deficit of creativity as we age? There are many reasons, but one of the most important is that as adults, we don't want rocket ships or castles. We want creative ideas that can be immediately implemented as innovations to products, services, or processes. Refining creative energy to produce what we want is much trickier than simply dreaming things up.

In my many years of coaching people toward innovation, I have found it very helpful to break down the creative process into smaller stages. Looking at the building blocks of innovation one by one makes the overall procedure less daunting. It helps us identify and build on our strengths as well as pinpoint and develop our weaknesses.

Unlike other activities, however, the creative process is not typically a linear progression that can be clearly defined in a particular number of steps, each naturally proceeding from the previous one. Rather, it is much more like a web in which various stages overlap and feed off of one another. So remember that as we discuss each phase of the creative process— creativity, creative power, and the power of creation— it is not uncommon to operate in each of the three phases simultaneously. However, the more you understand how each phase works, the better you will be able to maximize both your creative power and the resulting power of what you create. (In the next chapter, we will discuss the specific processes involved in each phase in much more detail.)

Creativity and the Brain

Creativity takes place in the brain. The brain is an organ, and creativity is profoundly affected by the balance of chemical messengers traveling in and out of your brain. If you or a loved one has ever suffered from depression, you undoubtedly understand that it is very difficult, if not impossible, to be creative when your brain is low on certain chemicals.

As professor and neuroeconomist Baba Shiv explained in *Stanford Business*, "Research shows that the best way to maximize creativity is to maintain high levels of both serotonin and dopamine, which will keep a person calm but energized."[1] Serotonin is a neurotransmitter that regulates mood, as well as some digestive and sexual functions. Low levels of serotonin are associated with depression. Dopamine is another neurotransmitter that controls the brain's pleasure and rewards system. Low levels of dopamine are associated with Parkinson's disease and a tendency toward addiction. When we have healthy levels of dopamine and serotonin, we feel excited, enthusiastic, and encouraged, and feel full of hope and possibility.

Fear and stress, on the other hand, release hormones such as cortisol, which inhibits the creative process. These chemicals create a neurological state known as arousal, more popularly termed the "fight-or-flight" response. This response was absolutely vital to our ancestors' survival when they needed the extra burst of energy either to run from a saber-toothed tiger or fight it off. Unfortunately for modern humans, these same hormones flood our bloodstream when the "threat" we face is an angry boss or a crashing hard drive. We are then left with a kind of energy ill-suited to help us solve problems.

The brain's entire focus when it is in this arousal state is to find safety. It looks for ways to minimize risk, which works against creativity and innovation. This is why leaders who use fear tactics to motivate their employees will see dismal results if their tasks requires any kind of creative thinking. It is also why fear of failure or competition (on an individual or organizational level) can cripple innovative potential. (We'll discuss this in more detail in Chapter 4.)

For decades, conventional wisdom has assumed that the left side of the brain is associated with systematic, analytical thinking, and the right brain with more creative, holistic thinking. For years people bought books and attended seminars on how to tap into right-brain thinking in order to become more creative. But reality is a little more complicated than that.

Recent advances in neuroimaging have allowed scientists to test these popular theories, and as a result, new evidence has emerged. In short, problem-solving and much of what we call creativity arises from both spheres of the brain. For example, math skills like counting and multiplication tables utilize the left brain while estimating size originates in the right.[2] Thus the challenge is not so much to access "right-brain thinking" or make a certain portion of our brains more dominant. Instead, we should look for healthy ways to keep serotonin and dopamine levels high enough while minimizing the fight-or-flight response.

Cultivating Creativity

Legendary choreographer Martha Graham once explained the artist's responsibility to cultivate creativity this way:

> There is a vitality, a life force, an energy, a quickening that is translated through you into action, and because there is only one of you in all of time, this expression is unique. And if you block it, it will never exist through any other medium and it will be lost. The world will not have it. It is not your business to determine how good it is nor how valuable nor how it compares with other expressions. It is your business to keep it yours clearly and directly, to keep the channel open. You do not even have to believe in yourself or your work. You have to keep yourself open and aware to the urges that motivate you.[3]

Graham sees creativity not as an itemized checklist but as a mental state. So how do we follow her advice and "keep the channel open"? Because the brain is a physical organ, there are many things—both physical and mental—that we can do to encourage and protect the creative state. The best news about these techniques and principles for cultivating creativity is that they work for everyone. You do not have to be a large company paying millions of dollars to Ivy League graduates to make the most of the creative potential that lies within the minds you and your employees already have.

- *Purge negative and fearful thoughts*: As we've already covered, stress is the physiological opposite of creativity. It is only natural to experience stress and fear in the course of a normal life. However, these emotions are toxic to the creative process and must be released before you can expect to utilize your creative energies effectively. Find ways to clear your mind of negative or stressful thoughts, whether it is through meditation, yoga, journaling, or even therapy.

- *Reframe your stress:* Reframing is the act of assigning new meaning to anything that feels threatening or stressful to us. Stress is often caused by our mental projections into an imaginary future. If we allow our imaginations to frame our future circumstances as harmful and attach negative emotions to them, then voilà: we feel stress! If we consciously reframe that same set of circumstances as a potential opportunity to open new doors or learn something new, our brains begin producing serotonin more efficiently than any medication.

- *Step into bright sunlight*: Exposure to bright sunlight has been shown to increase serotonin levels in the blood.[4] Take a walk or a jog in the sun or hold a meeting outside. During the winter months, or in climates unsuited to outdoor activities, consider using sunlight supplement lamps for a limited time each day.

- *Try something new*: New experiences are vital to awakening and strengthening the creativity in our brains. Individuals can try a mental activity like chess or crossword puzzles, or a hobby like painting or woodworking. Teams can try a group class or activity together. Learning a new skill—even if that skill is completely unrelated to what you are trying to accomplish—will force you to awaken parts of the brain that you do not normally use.

- *Eat well*: A healthy diet with proper levels of protein is also associated with healthy serotonin levels.[5] This doesn't mean you cannot indulge in junk food now and then, but just be aware of the need to fuel your brain.

- *Consume creativity*: Many business leaders read only business books, but you need to broaden your mind by wandering periodically into other fields. Whether it is reading literature, history, science, going to an art museum, or attending a play or poetry reading, be sure to give your mind opportunities to ingest the creativity of others. This also creates new neuronal connections that allow the mind to associate thoughts and ideas that were previously isolated from one another; such connections trigger heightened levels of creativity.

- *Make time for music*: Picking up your childhood musical instrument again, or even trying a new one for the first time, can offer your brain a real workout. Multiple studies have linked practicing a musical instrument to increased mental performance.[6]

- *Perform acts of kindness:* Both receiving and performing acts of kindness have a positive effect on the giver and receiver. Even witnessing an act of kindness can create a very similar effect. We have so many opportunities during any given day to be kind to others. Sometimes it is just a pleasant smile or remark, we may offer tangible help to somebody in need.

- *Get enough sleep*: Sometimes when the creative juices are flowing you may be up all night, perhaps several nights in a row. But as a general rule, your brain needs sufficient high-quality sleep to function at its best.[7]

- *Exercise*: Physical activity is not only vital to physical health, but also to mental health. It releases dopamine and serotonin, while ridding your body of stress hormones that hamper creativity.

- *Cultivate creative relationships*: As we discussed in the last chapter, collaboration can be an incredibly powerful ingredient in the creative process. Writing in the *Atlantic*, Joshua Wolf Shenk dispels the myth of the lone creative genius, explaining, "Competition and collaboration are often entwined. Only when we explore this terrain can we grasp how such pairs as Steve Jobs and Steve Wozniak, William and Dorothy Wordsworth, and Martin Luther King Jr. and Ralph Abernathy all managed to do such creative work. The essence of their achievements . . . was relational."[8]

- *Manage your emotions*: Make sure you are effectively managing any negative emotions. As we already discussed, depression is a chemical imbalance in the brain that makes it almost impossible to be creative. If you are suffering from depression or uncontrolled stress, be sure to seek treatment.

■ *Stay curious*: The rigid thinking we discussed in Chapter 1 is rooted in a desire for certainty in an uncertain world. Only when we embrace ambiguity will our creative potential be released. Columbia University neuroscientist Stuart J. Firestein, in his 2012 book, *Ignorance: How it Drives Science*, called the process of scientific discovery ". . . feeling around in dark rooms, bumping into unidentifiable things, looking for barely perceptible phantoms."[9]

Ambiguity and uncertainty awaken curiosity in scientists and drive investigation and discovery. By becoming curious about what we *do not* know, we push to expand what we *do* know.

To a curious mind, answers lead only to more questions. It is completely natural for uncertainty to arouse feelings of anxiety and frustration. However, in order to create the right environment for that creative spark to catch fire, we need to cultivate a tolerance of a level of uncertainty, reminding ourselves what we don't know and exploring it with curiosity. (We will talk about this in greater detail later in the book.)

Harnessing Creative Power

Of course being in a heightened state of creative energy is all fine and well, but what do we hope to gain from it? What end product should we expect from that curious mind and those heightened levels of serotonin and dopamine? Perhaps we all imagine emerging from such a state with fully complete plans for a product prototype or a marketing campaign. And in the case of creative exercises designed for a specific purpose, this may be possible.

But if your overall goal is to lay the groundwork for innovation—on an individual or organizational level—then you are looking for original ideas that are related to what you do. As we discussed in the last chapter, these ideas could be related to what you actually sell, how you make it, package it, market it, or deliver it. Harnessing creative power means taking the formless and unarticulated creative energy and using it to produce an idea that ultimately becomes something tangible and real.

Bruce Nussbaum, professor of Innovation and Design at Parsons at The New School of Design, has identified five core competencies of creative intelligence.

1. *Knowledge Mining*: Connecting information from a variety of sources in new ways.

2. *Framing*: Understanding how your point of view differs from and compares to other people's.
3. *Playing*: The ability to explore risk and possibility in the context of a game.
4. *Making.* The desire and ability to create something tangible.
5. *Pivoting*: The ability to transition quickly between concepts and production.[10]

Harnessing creative power can be compared to harnessing potential energy and turning it into kinetic energy: potential energy is stored up, waiting to be used; kinetic energy is energy of motion: doing work, accomplishing something. Nussbaum's first two competencies, Knowledge Mining and Framing, build up our storehouse of creative energy; Playing, Making, and Pivoting put that creativity to work to produce something new.

Many people have tried to come up with lists of steps you can take to put your creative energy to work. These might include activities like jotting down all your ideas on a paper, recording any spontaneous thoughts that hit you throughout the day, and setting aside dedicated time to think through your ideas. There is nothing wrong with this advice, but a set of static, linear steps runs contrary to the way that your brain wants to work. It seems much more important to deepen our understanding of creative action (in

Nussbaum's words, "raising our Creative IQ") so that we can begin cooperating with our brains instead of working against them.

There are two extremely important factors that profoundly affect creative action and are greatly misunderstood: competition and constraints. Both of these are business realities, and in our weaker and more fearful moments, we wish we could get rid of them. But examined in a different light, they are gifts to the creative process. They help us focus by forcing us to think more clearly and prioritize.

When you are trying to figure out how to make your business more profitable, it is very easy to wish your competitors would go away. But in the grand scheme of things, competition drives innovation. One of the reasons we care about building a better mousetrap, marketing it better, or producing it more efficiently, is that we know our competitors are up at night trying to figure out the same thing. Just like in sports, strong competitors force us to improve our performance or be eliminated.

Unfortunately, our attitude toward competition often hinders creativity. When we approach the task of innovation as if there were a finite amount of creativity in the world, we will become secretive and overly protective of our ideas. This often prevents us from getting the feedback we need to evaluate and improve them. In larger companies, this toxic kind of "competition" can exist between individuals or even departments. If someone mentions an idea in a meeting and someone else picks it up and runs with it, the person who originally had the idea may become jealous or angry. But it is in the best interests of the company that the creative power be harnessed, regardless of who does it.

A study published recently in the *Journal of Applied Psychology* demonstrated the negative effects of a territorial corporate culture on creativity. It showed that people who communicate territorial control over their ideas receive less creative feedback from others.[11] Effectively leading an innovative organization requires cultivating an atmosphere where people are more concerned with productivity than egotistical gratification. It also requires a system that allows people to effectively collaborate as well as share credit for successes. Allow employees from any department to present short pitches for new innovations—in any of the innovation areas discussed in the last chapter—on a regular basis. Determine the right intervals to create excitement without distracting from ongoing tasks. Be sure to reward those who come up with ideas that you implement, especially with recognition and giving credit where credit is due.

At the end of the day, people who effectively harness creative power do not waste much time or energy worrying about someone stealing their ideas, because they do not see creativity as a finite well that will someday run dry. They believe that there are just as many good ideas in their future as there are in their past.

In addition to being driven to improve performance, many powerful and innovative companies take their cues from their competitors. They look at what competitors are doing and ask how they can do it better, market it better, or do it more efficiently. These kinds of innovation may not seem as glamorous as inventing something new from scratch, but they benefit the consumer and the innovator just as much.

Constraints, whether they are related to finances, personnel, or the known laws of physics, are another misunderstood blessing. There is a paradoxical relationship between freedom and creativity. On the one hand, if we do not feel mentally, emotionally, and logistically free to soar with our ideas, it is nearly impossible for us to create anything. As we've already discussed, this is particularly true if we are wrapped up in fear, stress, or depression. Yet the proverbial blank canvas does not necessarily help us harness creative power particularly well.

Part of the weakness of brainstorming that we touched on in Chapter 1 is that there are no boundaries on the workability of certain ideas. "Wacky" and "innovative" are not the same thing. The same problem arises for artists, authors, poets, and musicians, many of whom voluntarily impose boundaries on what they create in order to focus their energy.

Imagine being told to write a story that was completely original, but with absolutely no other specifications for the assignment. Would this complete absence of limitations cause you to sit down at your computer and crank out the great American novel? Or would you stare at your keyboard for hours, wondering where to start? You would probably get farther faster if you were given a few more constraints; for example, that the story had to be a romance, or a mystery, and it needed to involve a war or a kidnapping. Most of us are actually more creative when certain boundaries or constraints are imposed on us from the beginning.

Dr. Patricia Stokes, in her book *Creativity From Constraints: The Psychology of Breakthrough,* notes that there are four types of constraints that can be used strategically to promote creativity rather than hinder it: domain constraints, cognitive constraints, variability constraints, and talent constraints. In practical terms, domain constraints mean that it is easier to come up with workable creative ideas in one's "domain": areas in which one has specialized knowledge and expertise. Cognitive constraints relate to the limits of human knowledge and understanding: A product (or a marketing campaign) that no one understands is ineffective, even if it has a brilliant premise.[12]

Variability constraints are driven by challenges within the status quo. One of the reasons the ancient Romans were not particularly innovative (although they were excellent engineers) is that they had a nearly limitless supply of human labor in the form of slaves. The Black Death, on the other hand, led to a flurry of new labor-saving devices in Europe, simply because there were not enough people to do the work that needed to be done. The more regularly we are challenged, Dr. Stokes says, the more habitually variable we will be. If necessity is the mother of invention, comfort is its enemy.

Talent constraints are somewhat self-explanatory. You will struggle to compose a symphony if you cannot read music, and you will have trouble designing a bridge if you lack an understanding of higher mathematics. Some of us are clearly better suited to some endeavors than others. However, talent constraints are not as cut and dry as many believe them to be, as we will see in the next chapter.

Often the most important step in solving a problem—whether it is in product development, production, or marketing—is identifying the constraints you face. Some of these can be overcome (for example, financial constraints may be overcome with investment capital). But just as often, we can harness creative power more effectively when we embrace the constraints before us.

Musician Jack White praised time constraints on his power to compose, declaring, "Deadlines make you creative. If you have all the time in the world, that kills creativity. If everything is pre-planned, and the tables are all set—nothing's going to happen. Constriction forces us to create."[13] Both solo entrepreneurs and companies may find some self-imposed constraints helpful. Setting deadlines and sticking to them will often unleash greater creative energy than if you give yourself all the time in the world. The same goes for financial constraints. Edison didn't actually invent the light bulb, after all. He invented the *affordable* light bulb.

I coached a Chief Marketing Officer of a large global consumer goods company that was navigating both the challenges of an economic crisis and continuous encroachment on their market by white label products. (White labels are the store brand products that imitate well-known brands and undercut their prices.) We discussed the company's need to "innovate or die," and I challenged him to take bolder actions and make bolder requests of his department.

During the next presentation from his team members, he affirmed their concept, and then challenged them to do the same with half the budget! After the initial shock wore off, the results were astonishing. The team returned with a go-to-market model that was superior to what they had originally presented. The model harnessed new technologies in a way that nobody in the industry had ever done before. The success that followed far surpassed any other campaign in the history of the company as well as in the entire industry.

Leveraging the Power of Creation

Once you have your concrete idea, the path for what to do next diverges based on what type of innovation the idea points to. If you are launching a new product, it may be time to look at creating a prototype. This may involve you, the engineering or programing department, or a freelancer. The next step may be to conduct market research or create a business or marketing plan. Whatever the next step, the result will be a tangible, testable innovation.

Not everyone who creates something entirely new and truly innovative will successfully leverage the power of that creation. For example, tablet computers existed in fiction long before they existed in real life. (Perhaps the most famous example was the 1968 film *2001: A Space Odyssey.*) During the 1990s and 2000s, several companies from AT&T to Microsoft released various versions with differing capabilities. But it was not until Apple released the iPad in 2001 that a company was able to leverage the power of a tablet computer to create an entire line of applications and accessories linked to its product.

Ultimately leveraging the power of creation requires moving beyond a workable idea and on to obtaining the resources to enter or create a market, and even an entire consumer ecosystem, built around that idea. Many years ago, I remember thinking vividly about creating a fast food chain that specialized in baked potatoes, offering a variety of toppings. This was clearly an actionable idea; if I had been serious about it, I could have done the research, drawn up a business plan, and sought capital through investments or loans. But the idea—although actionable and potentially profitable as a few regional chains like The Hot Potato and Potatopia have proven—was not the right idea for me to leverage at the time. I had no background in food service, nor did I really have any real desire to enter the field. So I did not pursue it.

We can leverage the power of creation when the creative idea we generate overlaps with our resources (or access to resources), abilities, and interests. Unfortunately, just because an idea gets funded does not mean it should be. Between 1997 and 2000, hundreds of millions of dollars of investment capital was poured into countless new technology companies. Because many of these companies were not turning a profit—and failed to do so even after huge infusions of cash—the infamous "tech bubble" burst, wreaking havoc on the U.S. economy.

It is easy to think that a great innovation will automatically become profitable, but it is important to remember that creating something that is genuinely original is a separate skill from making it profitable and scaling up production and distribution. Larger companies assign these tasks to different people or departments.

Although harnessing creative power is often a dynamic and exhilarating process, leveraging the power of creation typically involves more planning, calculation, and analysis. Besides the obvious moves like obtaining patents, domain names, trademarks and copyrights, you may want to look for other ways to leverage the intellectual property associated with your innovation. For authors, this includes securing rights to screenplays and translations into foreign languages. For a new product, it may include proactively publishing manuals and other information about how to best use the product. You may create a licensing system or form strategic partnerships with other companies to increase your distribution or reach.

Creative power and the power of creation are not random, spontaneous processes that are completely out of our control. We can take steps each day to cultivate an internal environment that primes our brains to produce greater creative power. We can research, plan, and work with those around us to ensure that we leverage what we create to its fullest potential. In Chapter 4, we'll examine how we can do all these things in a way that maximizes the creative momentum we experience.

Four

The Success Spiral

SEVERAL YEARS AGO, I was hired by a leading multinational consumer goods company that specialized in household, healthcare, and personal products, to coach an employee named Bernardo. An extremely successful marketing director, Bernardo had been promoted to a top managerial position in a Latin American business unit. They had offered him this three-year assignment in hopes that he could turn the company's sales around in the face of some significant challenges. If he succeeded, he would be guaranteed an even bigger executive leadership position in the near future.

Bernardo made the move to the country full of energy and anticipation. He had notebooks full of ideas and enthusiasm to spare. Unfortunately, after two years, very few of his ideas had had the intended effect. Sales remained stagnant and in some cases actually declined slightly. When the executive leadership noticed, they performed a complete reorganization of the management team, which included moving him out of the position.

Bernardo was devastated, but in reality, his bosses were not unhappy with him in particular; in fact, they relocated him to the central office and reassigned him to different tasks with a broader global impact. The problem was, up to that point in his career, everything Bernardo touched turned to gold. After being faced with what he saw as his first significant failure, he hardly knew who he was.

Failure is rarely a pleasant experience. No matter how often we read inspiring anecdotes about the failed prototypes Thomas Edison created or how many game-winning shots Michael Jordan missed, we never look forward to failing ourselves. At best, we try to push such experiences to the back of our minds and move on. At worst, we become like Bernardo, questioning our ability to perform and contribute.

Just as the artist's clothes are splattered with paint, the life of the bold mind is inevitably littered with failure. It is unrealistic to expect that every time we harness creative power the results will end up being everything we had hoped for. We cannot hope to be free of failure, but we can cultivate our creative momentum so that such failures do not impede our journey to success.

Understanding the Success Spiral

Success (or failure) is shaped not only by our experiences, but also by how we interpret and respond to those experiences. As you can see from Image 4-1 on page 78, the success spiral starts with accessing our potential. Author Stephen Covey distinguishes between mental and physical creation, referring to the former as "first creation" and the latter as "second creation." The more potential we access, the greater the "first creation" (the idea we come up with) will be. Then we take action to convert the first creation into the second creation (the innovation itself). As we've already covered, the innovation could be a product, service, production method, marketing concept, or anything else that gives the company a competitive edge. After the innovation has been launched, our brains create reference points based on the experience. If the second creation is successful, those reference points support empowering beliefs. Those beliefs allow us to access greater potential and thus create an even greater idea during the next cycle. If the second creation is a failure, the reference point created tends to reinforce limiting beliefs. Such beliefs can decrease the amount of potential we are able to access in the next cycle.

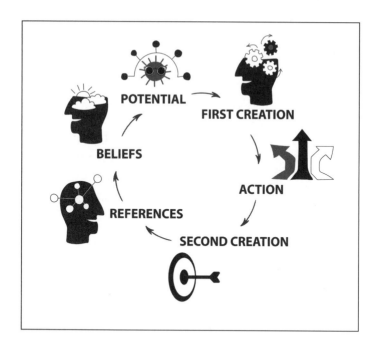

We intuitively understand the success spiral in other aspects of life. We see a basketball team get "in the zone" when each shot a player makes infuses his teammates with more confidence and excitement. We understand that when you make money, you can reinvest it to make more money. We know that if we care for our relationships, our friends will introduce us to others. But how does this kind of "success spiral" work with creativity?

Given the right conditions, creativity can grow and spread. Creative ideas from one person can infuse coworkers with the same excitement and confidence that a basket or a touchdown gives a player's teammates. In the right environment, creativity can fuel itself and awaken a spark in others.

In the creative success spiral, accessing potential produces an ongoing stream of unique and authentically new ideas (first creation). Those ideas are then developed into reality (second creation) and, by leveraging the power of creation, creators are able to reach new, previously unthinkable levels of innovation, attract more talent to the organization, and of course increase profitability. They also create positive reference points that reinforce empowering beliefs, thus allowing creators to access greater potential in the future. The better we understand the inherent challenges of these processes and the transitions between them, the more effectively we can keep the spiral moving in the right direction.

So how do we cultivate creative momentum in the face of challenges? Anyone who has attempted to launch a product or even a marketing campaign knows that there will always be obstacles beyond anyone's control. Ultimately, some first creation ideas that seemed great will not make it to second creation. Of those that do, not all will be leveraged successfully. Unless handled correctly, these kinds of setbacks can hamper future success.

The success spiral can stall for any number of reasons. Technical problems or misunderstandings can cause second creations to fade out. Misjudgments of the market or incorrect predictions about consumer needs can do the same. Sometimes a competitor—even a technically inferior one—seems to have better luck. Almost everyone agrees that Betamax was a superior product to VHS, yet the latter dominated the home video market for years before falling to the DVD.

President John F. Kennedy famously said of the disastrous Bay of Pigs invasion, "Victory has a thousand fathers, but defeat is an orphan." Yet sometimes failure really is no one's fault. It is just part of how life works. But we can choose whether we focus on the positive or the negative reference points moving forward. It is how we handle failure in all its forms that will determine whether we spiral upward or downward in the future.

Bernardo had not done anything wrong during his Latin American assignment. Customers just didn't respond to the campaigns he rolled out. That, combined with the country's economic situation, had led his bosses to believe that his talents could be better utilized in the central organization instead of a specific market.

After we began working together, Bernardo was put in charge of some of the company's most important brands whose sales were in decline. After I coached him through the application of specialized techniques to help him focus on his positive references, which support empowering beliefs and increase potential, he was able to not only halt the decline, but also to turn them around almost completely. He then leveraged the power of those creations to demand a much more talented team around him, access to even more R&D department time, and direct interaction with the senior management of the company. It took some time, but Bernardo finally realized that being reassigned was not a sign that he was no longer skilled or valuable; it was a blessing that enabled him to do much more for the company than he would have otherwise. (We will look at some of the specific techniques I used with Bernardo and many of my other clients in later chapters.)

The Downward Spiral

The downward spiral in business can be quite dramatic. In the case of Borders, discussed in Chapter 1, the company dove deeper into a business model that was rapidly becoming obsolete. The more committed they became to brick and mortar stores, the more debt they accrued, making it impossible to pivot when they needed to.

But as problematic as rising costs can be, cost-cutting can spur a downward spiral as well. A medium-sized real estate brokerage laid off support staff during a market downturn, surviving with only a receptionist to keep costs low. Nine months later they were given the opportunity to take on 30 new bank foreclosures—enough to keep their agents busy for more than a year. Unfortunately, because they had no one on staff trained to handle this volume of business, they couldn't accept the work without significantly compromising their performance.

In the creative process, the downward spiral is typically associated with how we approach the inevitable failures that come with innovation. When an idea does not materialize the way that we had hoped or when we cannot seem to solve a design problem or formulate a workable business model, it is natural to experience feelings of disappointment and even discouragement. This is exactly what happened to Bernardo during his Latin American assignment.

If you cannot effectively confront these feelings and refocus on your positive references, you will find yourself subconsciously taking steps to avoid them in the future. The result is an ongoing retreat in the creative process. Your next ideas will be less bold or "safer," where the outcome seems easier to predict or control. There is nothing inherently wrong with a safer idea, but this can easily lead to a pattern of becoming less and less innovative. Soon it begins to stifle creative power and will eventually snuff it out altogether.

Remember that creativity flourishes with the right chemical balance in the brain. When we react to failure with fear or panic, we enter into the "fight-or-flight" state in which our mind focuses on minimizing risk. From the outside looking in, it seems foolish that companies like Borders and Kodak—when faced with disruptive innovations—would retreat into doing what they had always done. But that is exactly what fear causes us to do. Old patterns are both comfortable and comforting, and that is what our brains want when they are full of cortisol and other stress hormones.

There are countless popular quotes about how failure is an integral part of success. Yet repeating those quotes does not necessarily prevent those destructive chemical changes in our brains or cause us to view failure in a productive way. Despite an entire "motivational" industry devoted to persuading us that chanting a few affirmations will fix all our problems, repeated studies have shown that reality is a little more complicated.

In fact, research suggests that simply repeating affirmations can actually be harmful for people who are suffering from depression or anxiety. Researchers argue that when such statements conflict deeply with an individual's underlying self-perception, they can actually reinforce that negative viewpoint, rather than correct it.[1] Such an overly simplistic approach often encourages us to deny or suppress negative thoughts rather than confront and change them. In order to avoid the downward spiral, we have to be able to correct our underlying beliefs about ourselves and what failure actually means.

Understanding and Preventing the Downward Spiral

As we've seen, many great artists and performers view the creative force as something great and limitless outside of themselves. Rather than being something finite that they are born with, they see creativity as an infinite resource that is greater than they are. Their task, then, is to open themselves up to this force and remove any obstacles that prevent them from receiving it.

Whatever one's metaphysical understanding of creativity, we would do well to examine the implications of this kind of worldview. First of all, as we alluded to in the last chapter, such an understanding places control of (and responsibility for) one's creativity firmly in the hands of the individual. If an endless supply of creativity is available to you, you can't use the excuse that you "aren't creative enough" or that you "can't seem to think of any good ideas." Instead the question becomes, "What is blocking my creative energy, and what can I do to remove that blockage?"

In fact, whether we believe traits like creativity are fixed and finite or infinite and developable has been shown to have a great deal of influence over our performance. Dr. Carol Dweck, a psychologist at Stanford University, has conducted years of research into how what we believe about ourselves affects our achievements and well-being. She has learned that if we believe qualities such as talent, intelligence, and creativity are inborn, static qualities, we will shy away from challenges and development. On the other hand, if we view these qualities as developable, then we will work harder and handle setbacks more productively.

Dweck refers to the first outlook as the "fixed" mindset and the second as the "growth" mindset.

Dweck's research has profound implications for how we respond to failure. As she explains in her book *Mindset: The New Psychology of Success*, "In one world—the world of fixed traits—success is about proving you're smart or talented. Validating yourself. In the other—the world of changing qualities—it's about stretching yourself to learn something new. Developing yourself. In one world, failure is about having a setback. Getting a bad grade. Losing a tournament. Getting fired. Getting rejected. It means you're not smart or talented. In the other world, failure is about not growing. Not reaching for the things you value. It means you're not fulfilling your potential."[2]

Dweck also points out that the belief in the idea of inborn genius holds a great deal of romantic appeal for most of us and can be very difficult to excise from our subconscious thinking. It is very tempting to think that we are inherently better—more talented, more intelligent, more creative—than others. Movies and books celebrate the narrative of the exceptional individual who was obviously special from a young age, whether it is a sports figure, political leader, or an artist. But as attractive as this idea is, it is ultimately destructive to our growth and performance.

Many positive affirmations can unintentionally reinforce the fixed mindset by suggesting that we are inherently intelligent or somehow destined for greatness. However, if we accept this view, failure becomes a threat to our identity rather than merely an opportunity for learning and growth. This is what initially happened to Bernardo; he was so devastated by the failure of his ideas that he hardly knew who he was anymore.

Smooth Transitions

Each component of the creative process presents its own obstacles, but the transition between stages can be particularly challenging. The transition from first creation to second creation often involves a fair amount of risk. This is the point at which we must decide what resources—both money and manpower— to invest, and how long we will continue to try until it works or we give up. It requires careful cost/benefit analysis, but also decisive action.

In order to make the right decisions when transitioning between first and second creation, we must understand that sometimes the risk of doing nothing actually outweighs the risk of failure. When we fail to act on ideas in a productive way, we risk contributing to the downward spiral and reducing the number of creative ideas we generate in the future. This holds true for the solo entrepreneur and the large company.

Business leaders from Milton Hershey to Bill Gates watched their first companies fail before becoming the spectacular successes we are so familiar with today.

Truly innovative companies create a mandate to "fail quickly" in the second creation stage. Leaders of such companies embrace failure as a source of growth and learning and do not stigmatize it. They realize that any time you are trying to do something authentically new, you will inevitably create some innovations that do not work as hoped.

Unfortunately, as with many business trends, other companies that claim to embrace failure are merely paying lip service to the idea. They still put as much pressure as ever on their employees to avoid failure at all costs and succeed as quickly and flawlessly as possible. Rather than spur innovation, this approach often incentivizes shortcuts that give the superficial impression of success to investors or senior management.

Not long ago the digital world was inundated with "growth hackers," professionals who promised to use all sorts of sophisticated methods of analysis to boost exposure and sales quickly. Unfortunately, for the less scrupulous, growth hacking also involved artificially inflating results by purchasing likes, followers, and other indicators of social media popularity and reach. This is really nothing new, of course. For years, authors have purchased copies of their own books through various means in order to be placed on the best-seller list, and continue to do so today.

But the questionable legality and ethics behind such short cuts distracts from the underlying reality that they obscure. After all, purchases and referrals do more than just bring in revenue; they communicate whether or not customers are actually being served by the innovation itself. As Rob Asghar writes in *Forbes*, "If you have a genuine commitment to embracing failure and learning from it, you won't feel a need to take shortcuts. You would even be repulsed by shortcuts, as they introduce noise into the process of figuring out what works and what doesn't work."[3]

Innovative companies understand that "fail fast" doesn't mean fail on purpose. It means creating a smooth transition between first and second creation, and producing more workable second creations with an acceptable margin of risk. Larger companies can dedicate specific departments to these tasks, because they can afford to fund some mistakes as well as ideas that take longer to become profitable. Solo entrepreneurs will need to set aside a portion of the budget and work within it.

The other advantage to failing quickly is the ability to gather data points on the path to a solution. Thomas Edison famously declared, "I haven't failed. I've just found 10,000 ways that don't work." This sounds extreme, but it is exactly how scientific research is conducted all the time. New drug therapies and other treatments would never be developed if scientists were not allowed to eliminate dozens or even hundreds of possibilities that don't end up working.

In fact, the transition between stage one and stage two can best be thought of as a time for experimentation, in which we obtain as much data as we can from every success and failure. One of the greatest examples of this kind of bold new experimentation is happening (as of this writing) with a revolutionary partnership between Oracle Team USA—the America's Cup winning sailing team—and Airbus, one of the world's leading manufacturers of airplanes.

While sailing and flying seem inherently very different, Airbus's engineers are hard at work helping design a radically different racing sailboat. As the company explained on its website, "As the team's Official Innovation Partner, Airbus is sharing the know-how of its experts in areas that include aerodynamics, instrumentation, simulation, composites, structures, hydraulics and data analysis. In parallel, Airbus benefits from the innovative approach of a world leader in sailing technology in their quest to retain the America's Cup. 'The Cup' is arguably one of the most difficult trophies to win in the world of sport—and the oldest sports trophy of the modern era (dating back to 1851)."[4]

Prototypes in the works right now utilize a rigid mainsail, which has a great deal in common with a plane wing. They also fly above the water, rather than in it, reducing friction and moving at two to four times the speed of the wind. Airbus has effectively leveraged the power of their creation to reach previously unimaginable levels of creativity, and what they learn in the partnership process accelerates their own Airbus R&D.

This is how we optimize the shape of the wing at Airbus...

Experimentation and assessment are necessary to drive the innovation process forward. But this doesn't have to occur on a scale as grand as the Oracle/Airbus partnership. Experimentation can involve something as simple as developing prototypes that are only partially complete and having a client fund the remainder of the development, therefore sharing the risk.

If the trick for maintaining momentum between first and second creation is to allow for adequate experimentation and course correction, then the secret to maintaining momentum between second creation and re-accessing potential is to leverage the creation effectively without becoming trapped by its success. This is where we see the upward spiral really take off.

The Upward Spiral

The recipe for the upward spiral will vary from company to company, but some of the ingredients are essential. Besides a productive view of failure and smooth transitions between components of the creative process, a powerful driving vision and accompanying determination are found in almost every leader who successfully innovates throughout a period of time.

In his memoir, *Pour Your Heart Into It*, Starbucks CEO Howard Schultz describes growing up in poverty and then working his way through college. Schultz wanted more out of a job than just the financial stability or even the wealth that had eluded him during his childhood. He wanted to do something he was deeply passionate about.

Schultz initially encountered Starbucks as the leader of a sales team for the company that sold them their drip coffee makers. After purchasing the company, he expanded the chain from three stores to more than 21,000 worldwide, driven by an experience he had overseas when he saw the relationship Italian patrons had with their local coffee shops.

But Starbucks's meteoric rise—and that of its CEO—was not without its setbacks. Schultz actually left the company early on—before later returning and purchasing it—because the senior management rejected his Italy-inspired vision. Schultz's initial attempts to obtain investment capital were rejected hundreds of times. During its rapid expansion, Starbucks's quality began to decline and sales began to flag. Schultz also bought the Seattle Supersonics, a move that ended in the disastrous and unpopular sale of the team and its move to Oklahoma City. But Schultz's passion for what he did would not allow these failures to send him into a downward spiral. As he explained to the *New York Times* in a 2010 interview, "If you don't love what you're doing with unbridled passion and enthusiasm, you're not going to succeed when you hit obstacles."[5]

Schultz also focused on making Starbucks a desirable place to work, recognizing that another crucial element of the upward spiral is attracting and keeping the right people. Not long ago I spoke with the leader of a group of engineers who run flight tests for a well-known airline. He explained that his group was charged with placing thousands of sensors on every imaginable part of the airplane during flight tests in order to measure wind speed, air pressure, temperature, and other important variables related to the plane's performance.

While they conducted this needed research, they were under tremendous pressure to innovate. And indeed, a few of the engineers had developed a cheaper sensor that more accurately measured some of the variables they were most interested in. However, the atmosphere in the department was tense and anxious, and many talented engineers were leaving for greener pastures when opportunities arose.

What if the company, instead of pressuring its engineers to come up with innovations against very tight deadlines, offered meaningful incentives to do so? Again, the chemical response of the brain with the possibility of gain is so much different from its response to the fear of great loss. Leaders of innovative companies understand that creative energy is a resource like anything else. You'll often get better results by offering extra time and rewards rather than pressure.

Another great way to build the momentum in the spiral is to consistently leverage the power of the company's existing creations while always thinking about how to expand and diversify. When Disney acquired Pixar in 2006, it didn't just allow Pixar to operate with a larger budget. The acquisition energized the rest of the company. Not only have its Pixar offerings remained reliable box office hits, but non-Pixar films like *Frozen* have become some of its highest grossing movies of all time.

The collaboration of Airbus and Oracle Team USA represents a completely unexpected and potentially disruptive collaboration, utilizing the technology of one industry in another that isn't obviously related. Leveraging the power of your creation in unexpected ways increases not only your profits but also the scope of possibilities for the future. The upward spiral is characterized not only by funding research and development, but also by this kind of increased communication, collaboration, and ultimately impact on the world at large.

Here are other actions that keep the success spiral spinning upward.

- *Choosing creativity over control*: Traditionally, purchasing companies have dismantled the companies they acquire, eliminating duplicate positions and folding the remaining employees into the parent organization. But simply expanding staff and market share—even if the added individuals are incredibly talented and creative—is not necessarily a recipe for great innovation. Innovative companies making acquisitions are now taking a more hands-off approach. For example, when Facebook acquired Instagram in 2012 and WhatsApp in 2014, it allowed both companies to function as autonomous subsidiaries within the larger company.
- *Purging*: Most educators and artists acknowledge the need for periodic mental

and even spiritual cleansing in order to create room for new ideas. This process can be compared to a data dump from the hard drive of a computer to make room for new information. The U Theory, developed by Otto Scharmer, posits that the linear approach to building on the past leads us to repeat our previous results over and over. Instead of a straight line, he views the path to innovation as a "U," in which we go deeply down into ourselves, and then emerge with fresh new ideas. To create a truly new and innovative future, he explains, we must work toward keeping a truly open mind, open heart, and open will.[6]

There are many different techniques to accomplish this. Some people "mind dump" into their journals or digital voice recorders. Others download a conversation to a group or mentor. Still others find meditation (covered more extensively in later chapters) to be a helpful technique. Whatever you need to do to quiet and empty yourself of all the mental clutter will help you make room for creativity.

- *Building authentic confidence*: Authentic confidence is like a muscle, strengthened through time by a track record of real achievements. When you build this kind of resume for yourself, you are investing in your future success. If the brain enters the fight or flight response, it is very easy to forget all the times in the past that you have overcome obstacles. Have a way to remind yourself of all the times you found solutions to problems that seemed impossible. Keep these positive references for your company as well. Confidence based on real past experiences enables you to take the bold, decisive actions necessary to keep the spiral going.

- *Evaluating effectively*: Making the most of every failure and success requires determining exactly why the failures did not work, and why the successes did. Only by investigating with genuine curiosity and diligently recording your findings can you use the information to avoid the same mistakes and repeat the successes. This also requires formulating clear metrics for evaluation and sticking to them. Don't ever stop measuring what you're doing to determine if you're really getting the results you want.

- I coach executives to spend much more time analyzing successes. If we really want to accelerate success we have to become true "students of success." After all, you don't learn much about wealth by studying poverty or much about health by studying disease. In the same way, you don't become an expert on success by studying failure.

- *Correcting course*: Evaluation doesn't only occur after an innovation has launched. Ongoing evaluation enables you to face both good and bad news early and act decisively in response. In 2008, Starbucks sales were slumping after a period of legendary expansion. Schultz diagnosed the problem and responded by closing more than 7,000 U.S. stores for three and a half hours in order to retrain its staff to make drinks properly. Despite the nationwide recession, sales and stock prices strongly rebounded.[7]

- *Cultivating right relationships*: As we discussed in Chapter 3, jealousies over who gets credit can be toxic to the creative process. Cultivate an atmosphere in which everyone is excited for the same mission and feels confident that credit will be given where it is due. Don't let tensions linger; confront any misunderstandings and resolve them quickly. Preserving creative chemistry is worth it.

- *Maintaining the growth mindset*: As we've established, your brain's chemical balance is vital to maintaining creative energy.

Condition your mind to focus on your positive references and your emotions to respond productively to both failure and success. Failure is not a mark against your worth as a person or the validity of your ideas, nor is success a validation of it. Both failure and success are opportunities to grow, to learn, and to gather data that would not have been available to you had you not tried. Learn to reframe experiences accordingly.

All these techniques sound simple, and most of them are. But they require a level of self-mastery that eludes most of us for our entire lives. In the next chapter, we'll explore keys to mastering our own minds.

Five

Mastering One's Mind

ONE OF THE MOST common ways we misunderstand creativity is by assuming it is somehow opposed to self-control. In movies and novels, creative people are often portrayed as quirky and unpredictable, living disorganized lives by their own rules and refusing to adhere to a daily schedule or conform to other societal expectations. Although there may certainly be a few highly creative people who fit this description, such characteristics are far from essential to the dynamic, creative mind. In fact, self-control and mental discipline actually increase creativity and improve its application. A bold mind is also a controlled mind.

Philosopher and mathematician Rene Descartes's famous revelation "Cogito ergo sum" (I think, therefore I am) has led many to misconstrue the mind as the seat of our essence or identity. However, we now know that the human brain is an organ—a highly complex, information-processing organ, to be sure—but a physical organ nonetheless. When we think about maximizing creative power and effectively harnessing the power of creation, it is perhaps most helpful to think of the mind as a tool at our disposal. Our level of mental discipline indicates our level of control over that tool. The better we master our own minds, the more effectively we will be able to use them to achieve our goals.

In his classic work *As A Man Thinketh*, James Allen writes, "A man's mind may be likened to a garden, which may be intelligently cultivated or allowed to run wild; but whether cultivated or neglected, it must, and will, bring forth. If no useful seeds are put into it, then an abundance of useless weed seeds will fall therein, and will continue to produce their kind."[1]

In short, the relative fertility or barrenness of our minds is a product of what we have planted in them and allowed to grow. Furthermore, a mind can be very active without producing what we want, just as a garden may be full of weeds. Just as weeds are much easier to remove if they are caught early, unproductive, wandering thoughts are easier to eliminate before they have grown into chronic distractions. Only when we have carefully pruned the gardens of our minds will their production begin to align with our goals.

But susceptibility to distraction does not mean that you do not possess the capacity to be deeply creative. In fact, just the opposite may be true. A study by Northwestern University published in *Neuropsychologia* found that highly creative people, including luminaries such as Marcel Proust and Charles Darwin, were more easily distracted than the average person, particularly by sensory stimuli such as sounds or lights. "The researchers hypothesized that this sensory hypersensitivity might contribute to creativity because it widens the individual's scope of attention. So, people who take in more information would be more likely to make new and unusual connections between diverse pieces of information."[2]

So for optimal creativity, we must strike a careful balance between openness and focus. Hyper-focus—the ability to shut out all distractions and focus completely on one task—is actually a symptom of Attention Deficit Hyperactivity Disorder (ADHD). This might seem counterintuitive, as we tend to think of ADHD sufferers as unable to focus. In reality, they struggle to control the subject of their focus; in short, they have difficulty regulating their attention.

If we are honest, most of us struggle to regulate our attention as consistently as we would like. We have productive periods of time, but then we have days on end where we go to bed dissatisfied with what we have accomplished. We stick to our diet for a while, but then the holidays come. We do well with our exercise program, but then a crisis hits and everything gets off track. How can we develop the kind of self-discipline that withstands the ups and down of life? This chapter will explore both the principles and skills needed to defeat distraction, focus on the task at hand, and ultimately make optimal use of our minds.

Four Energies

A growing number of scientists, thinkers, and leaders are concluding that, when it comes to productivity, time and money are not the only scarce resources we must conserve. Energy—whether it is physical, mental, emotional, or even spiritual—is perhaps even more vital to harnessing creativity and accomplishing our goals. The key to mastering our minds lies first in managing these energies effectively.

It's very easy to think about skills like focus as purely cognitive capacities. But a growing body of research is confirming what mystics and shamans have known for millennia: we are multidimensional beings with spirit, soul, mind, and body, all of which are deeply interconnected. Each part or layer influences and is influenced by each of the others. Thus the man who truly seeks to master his own mind cannot do so without mastering the rest of his being as well.

Many ancient religions held that these four components corresponded to what were viewed as the basic elements making up the physical world: Our bodies were earth, our emotions were water, our minds were air, and our spirits were fire. The goal in many pre-axial faiths was to keep all four elements healthy and in balance. When they were not, the individual would experience distraction and other unpleasant side effects.

Today in the West we are just beginning to rediscover this ancient wisdom and its relevance to our modern lives. In his book *The Corporate Athlete: How to Achieve Maximal Performance in Business and Life*, author Jack Groppel applies athletic training principles to the business world. The book details how we can cultivate and manage our physical, emotional, mental, and spiritual energy. As Groppel explains, "Human beings are biological organisms requiring sleep, nutrition, and activity to survive, let alone thrive. Every person needs to replenish energy in the form of sleep, nutrition, and activity, as well as emotional, mental, and spiritual recovery."[3]

Caring for our physical bodies is vital for both creativity—as we've covered in previous chapters—as well as for focus and overall performance. This naturally means a balanced, healthy diet with sufficient protein, complex carbohydrates, fresh fruits, vegetables, nuts, and seeds, as well as regular rigorous exercise. But Groppel offers more lessons from the science of sports performance that are relevant to the self-discipline necessary for creativity and business performance. He notes that several decades ago, world-class athletes typically trained for big events by putting in more hours with more rigorous repetitions. Although this technique did improve performance to a point, it also led to repetitive stress and even traumatic injuries as athletes over-fatigued their muscles and allowed themselves insufficient time to recover. Today, most elite athletes follow what is known as interval or periodic training; they alternate different muscle groups or activities, allowing their bodies to recover and preventing overuse.

The application of these principles moves beyond creating the physically ideal conditions for creativity and focus. Techniques for cultivating physical energy actually have implications for how we can effectively cultivate and focus our mental energy. Rigorous exercise actually causes micro-tears in muscle fibers, which then cause the fibers to heal stronger than they were before. In the same way, periods of intense mental exertion followed by periods of mental rest can leave our minds sharper and more fine-tuned to the task at hand. Rather than trying to concentrate intensely all the time, we can obtain better results by scheduling times for mental recovery into our routine. We can also alternate mentally demanding activities with those that require less concentration.

Emotional energy influences mental energy as well. As we have already discussed, healthy relationships are vital to optimizing creativity. So is overall emotional self-control. Writing in *Harvard Business Review*, Tony Schwartz and Catherine McCarthy explain, "When people are able to take more control of their emotions, they can improve the quality of their energy, regardless of the external pressures they're facing . . . they first must become more aware of how they feel [during] the workday and of the impact these emotions have on their effectiveness."[4]

In addition to meditation and deep breathing, Schwartz and McCarthy advocate regularly expressing gratitude and appreciation to others. They explain that this can be done in a handwritten note, an email, in person, or over the phone. The authors also demonstrate that such regular expressions of thanks have a positive effect on the giver as well as on the receiver of the gratitude.

Interestingly, the well-established link between attentional deficit and negative moods seems to cut both ways. In other words, not only does managing one's emotions improve one's focus, but improving one's ability to focus enhances one's overall emotional wellbeing. According to the study *Fixing Our Focus: Training Attention to Regulate Emotion* by Heather A. Wadlinger and Derek M. Isaacowitz, published in 2011, "[S]elective attention to positive information reflects emotion regulation, and that regulating attention is a critical component of the emotion regulatory process. Furthermore, attentional regulation can be successfully trained through repeated practice."[5]

The Elusive "Why"

The spiritual energy we need to cultivate and maintain effective focus does not need to be religious, although it certainly can be. In its simplest form, our spiritual energy is found in whatever motivates us to do what we do. Many people who may seem scattered or distracted in daily life become extremely focused in a crisis because the situation intensifies their motivation. When there is a fire in a building, no one is distracted from the primary task of getting outside to safety. When a child needs to be taken to the hospital, her mother is not thinking about the bills that need to be paid or the milk she forgot to pick up from the grocery store. But how can we find that kind of focus in everyday life?

Countless posters and internet memes urge everyone to "Know Your Why." They remind us that it is easier to focus on our goals when we are inspired by and connected to something larger than ourselves. Yet finding the intrinsic motivator that can help us regulate our attention can be a very different process for different people. We all know the "why's" that are supposed to motivate us (taking care of our loved ones, making the world a better place) but that does not mean we are deeply connected to a motivation that blocks out distraction and puts all of our other priorities in order.

Most psychologists divide an individual's motivation into two major categories: promotion focus and prevention focus. Promotion-focused individuals see goals as opportunities. They focus on the rewards that they will receive for their efforts and are comfortable with risk. Prevention-focused individuals see their goals as responsibilities and work to avoid risk and keep out of trouble. We commonly hear these two viewpoints expressed as "playing to win" versus "playing not to lose."

Although you may immediately conclude that promotion-focused individuals are more creative (and they are), it is important to recognize that prevention-focused individuals also bring advantages to the table. They tend to be more careful and precise. Although they may not generate a lot of new ideas, they can be excellent analysts and problem-solvers. Of course all of us are both promotion and prevention focused to some degree. Because promotion focus is associated with greater creativity and innovation, we want to be able to amplify our promotion focus as much as possible, without losing the positive qualities that prevention focus offers.

Interestingly—and perhaps somewhat counter-intuitively—possessing greater self-control is associated with greater promotion focus. According to a study by Tracy Cheung, Marleen Billebaart, Floor Korese, and Denise De Ridder, which investigated the link between happiness and greater self-control, individuals who demonstrated greater self-control were, "(1) more promotion-focused on acquiring positive gains thereby facilitating more approach-oriented behaviors, and (2) less prevention-focused on avoiding losses thereby reducing avoidance-oriented behaviors."[6]

Enemies of Focus

In his landmark book, *Thinking, Fast and Slow*, Nobel Prize-winning author Daniel Kahneman explains these two sides to our motivation in even greater detail. He proposes that it is best to think of our minds being composed of two systems: System 1 is our intuitive and instinctual mind, while System 2 is our rational, calculating mind. System 1 moves quickly and effortlessly, while System 2 moves slowly and requires huge amounts of energy.

Self-control is the territory of System 2, and exercising it is a tiring ordeal resulting in a drain known as "ego depletion." Kahneman cites the work of psychologist Roy Baumeister, who demonstrated that people who exert self-control in a situation—thus experiencing ego depletion—have less self-control for the next task set before them. Hence, someone who suppresses the urge to yell at a coworker might cheat on his diet later that day.

Kahneman goes on to explain, "[T]he idea of mental energy is more than a mere metaphor. The nervous system consumes more glucose than most other parts of the body. When you are actively involved in difficult cognitive reasoning or engaged in a task that requires self-control, your blood glucose level drops."[7]

So what is the difference between the individuals studied by Cheung who demonstrated self-control and also greater promotion focus and those studied by Baumeister who demonstrated ego depletion? Comparing the subjects of two different studies will always be like comparing apples and oranges, but clearly one set of subjects did not have to exert as much effort or energy to exercise the self-control the study required. This is exactly what happens when our brains automate processes: Whether it's exercising five times a week or rising early each day, the more habitual an act becomes, the less mental effort it takes. The individual who isn't in the habit of yelling at anyone won't need to exert energy to avoid yelling at his coworker (so it will be easier for him to stick to his diet).

The enemy of focus is distraction, which comes in two major forms: outward and inward. Outward distractions are often sensory, such as a noisy conversation at the next table or a thunderstorm outside. Inward distractions tend to be more emotional or spiritual. They are related to the inner dialogue that is constantly running in the background of our minds, stirring up everything from anticipation and excitement to fear and anger.

Outward distractions relate to the "sensory gating" in the thalamus portion of the brain, which filters out information that is not important or meaningful to us. If this "gate" is fairly narrow, people can work easily in a crowded room because their brains can effectively shut out all the extraneous noises. If the gate is wide, an individual may require almost complete silence and isolation to read or complete even a fairly straightforward task. In extreme cases, dysfunctional sensory gating is associated with conditions such as autism spectrum disorder and schizophrenia.

By contrast, our reticular activating system—or extrathalamic control modulatory system—tells our brains what to focus on. It's the reason that when you learn you're going to have a baby, you start seeing baby-related items everywhere. Those items were always there, you just never noticed them before. This region of the brain also causes you to recognize your baby's cry anywhere, even in a crowded, noisy room. We'll talk more about specific techniques to program your reticular activating system—and thus control what information your brain takes in—in Chapter 8.

Inward distractions relate to our stream of consciousness and inward thoughts. Many of us have experienced the sensation of our minds racing a mile a minute when we are trying to concentrate on a task or fall asleep at night. In extreme cases, such internal commotion can be associated with generalized anxiety disorder or other mental illnesses. So how do we calm these "inner voices" that not only prevent us from being productive and creative, but also from enjoying life?

Mindfulness, the practice of detaching oneself from one's thoughts and feelings and observing them objectively, has helped many people deal with wandering thoughts, particularly when they are anxious or stressful. Except in extreme crisis situations, when many people are able to think clearly and act decisively, anxiety and stress are directed at the past or the future. Why didn't I remember to make that phone call yesterday? How am I going to pay my mortgage next month? Mindfulness, by contrast, encourages us to stay in the present moment.

As Eckhart Tolle explains in his book, *The Power of Now: A Guide to Spiritual Enlightenment*, "Time isn't precious at all, because it is an illusion. What you perceive as precious is not time but the one point that is out of time: the Now. That is precious indeed. The more you are focused on time—past and future—the more you miss the Now, the most precious thing there is."[8] Directing our attention to something as simple and basic as our breathing or an awareness of our hands or feet can slow down anxious or distracting thoughts. Mindfulness is not an easy skill, but it can be improved with consistent practice.

Understanding Focus

In his book, *Focus: The Hidden Driver of Excellence* Daniel Goleman argues that singular hyper-focus, although necessary to accomplish certain tasks, should not be our chief goal as innovative leaders. Leaders must strive to cultivate what he calls a "triple focus": an ability to manage simultaneously our attention on the inner, the other, and the outer. The inner focus relates to our own self-awareness and self-management, the other focus relates to empathy for and understanding of what motivates other people—particularly those we are charged with leading—and the outer focus relates to the complex systems and broad patterns that make up our world.

Goleman emphasizes that it is where leaders direct their attention, much more than their specific words or instructions, that determines where their followers (and their organizations) will end up. In short, people will focus on whatever they perceive is most impor-tant to their leaders. Goleman carefully distinguishes between being driven to accomplish a goal, and being so focused on a goal (such as increasing a company's market share), that you will do anything—including hurting people and violating your own values and eth-ical standards—in order to achieve it.

He goes on to clarify, "Every organization needs people with a keen focus on goals that matter, the tal-ent to continually learn how to do even better, and the ability to tune out distractions. Innovation, productivity, and growth depend on such high-performers."[9] In other words, there is a difference between a creative person hyper-focusing on a particular task (harnessing creative power to build a prototype of a new product, for example) and an organization being so hyper-focused on profitability that they exhaust their best people and drive them away. As Goleman explains, "The key is finding balance, and knowing when to use the right kind of focus at the right time."

For most people, adjusting and strengthening focus is not a matter of lengthening attention span as it is managing one's attention more effectively. One of the most dangerous things in life is not to be unable to focus on anything for very long, but rather to be focused—even hyper-focused—on the wrong thing. As we discussed in the last chapter, if you focus on your mistakes, failures, and negative reference points, you will quickly generate a downward spiral toward more and more problems. But if you focus on your successes you will soon find yourself succeeding at even greater levels. We will discuss the mental toughness or resilience needed to accomplish this more in Chapter 8.

Perhaps one of the most helpful ways to train the mind to focus is with a mindfulness-based martial arts program. Regardless of the specific martial art (taekwondo, karate, aikido, and so on) the deep breathing, awareness skills, concentration skills, meditation, and visualization skills are all extremely helpful. Particularly in sparring, the emphasis of staying in the present moment can be very instructive in other areas of life. As the legendary Bruce Lee explained, "The great mistake is to anticipate the outcome of the engagement; you ought not to be thinking of whether it ends in victory or defeat. Let nature take its course, and your tools will strike at the right moment."[10] I have actually used martial arts sparring to instruct CEOs and other corporate leaders in focus and present-moment awareness with great success.

For those who struggle with a short attention span the problem is often a matter of learning to delay gratification. In the famous Marshmallow Test, researchers led by psychologist Walter Mischel at Stanford University tested children's ability to delay gratification by offering them a single marshmallow and then leaving the room. The children were told they could eat the single marshmallow right away, or if they were willing to wait for the adult to return, they would be rewarded with a second marshmallow. Researchers found that the children who could wait for the second marshmallow had better life outcomes, including higher SAT scores and overall educational and professional success.

Nearly 50 years since the original study was conducted, advancing research about the brain has told us even more about why some children waited for the second marshmallow and others didn't. Modern neuroimaging reveals that the prefrontal cortex (the area that controls executive function) is more animated in self-controlled individuals, while the ventral striatum (the area that controls desire) is more active in those who struggle with self-control.[11] Of course, some may not have possessed the self-control necessary to wait, while others did but chose not to use it.

But the experiment revealed more than just who possessed willpower and who didn't. Mischel's conclusion was not that the stronger-willed children prevailed, but rather the children who were able to allocate their attention in a way that suited their goals were successful. In other words, the children who were able to delay gratification didn't stare at the marshmallow and use their iron will to resist the temptation. They were able to find ways to ignore the marshmallow and think about something else. As Mischel explained, "Once you realize that will power is just a matter of learning how to control your attention and thoughts, you can really begin to increase it."[12]

One of the reverse behaviors of delaying gratification is procrastination, yielding to the temptation of doing something more enjoyable now and putting off a task that seems daunting or unpleasant. A study published by Laura Rabin, Joshua Fogel, and Katherine Nutter-Upham of Brooklyn College of the City University of New York, explored the relationship of executive function to procrastination. They write, "Procrastination is increasingly recognized as involving a failure in self-regulation . . . procrastinators . . .

may have a reduced ability to resist social temptations, pleasurable activities, and immediate rewards. . . . These individuals also fail to make efficient use of internal and external cues to determine when to initiate, maintain, and terminate goal-directed actions."[13]

Cultivating Mastery of our Minds

There are many practical ways to cultivate mastery of our own minds.

- *Identify unproductive habits and begin to work on them*: Habits cannot be turned around in a day or even a week. It is almost always more effective to identify them and work on them gradually. For example, suppose you know you need to work on waking up an hour earlier so you have time to meditate, begin an exercise program, improve your diet, and get to bed earlier. You could work on these all at once with small steps by adjusting your wake and bedtime by 10 minutes each, trying to drink one extra bottle of water each day, and committing to exercise for fifteen minutes three times this week. After a week you could increase each practice incrementally, rising a little earlier, going to bed a little earlier, adding a salad, and extending your exercise time. Or you could simply pick one of these habits and work on it until it is significantly improved and then move on to the next. Remember to reward yourself for success so that you have a positive association with that habit.

Don't forget that the end game of cultivating a habit is to make it automatic. You want the behavior to become so routine that you expend less energy doing it. In this way, cultivating good, healthy habits can be seen as investing a large amount of mental energy on the front end so that you can reap "mental energy" savings the rest of the your life.

- *Identify and minimize distractions*: This might seem like common sense, but it eludes a surprising number of professionals. Different things distract different people. Perhaps you can work in a crowded coffee shop, but you need to disable social media in order to concentrate. Pay attention to what distracts you during the day, and find ways to avoid or eliminate them.

- *Develop a focusing ritual*: In addition to regular prayer or meditation, develop a short ritual to refocus your attention throughout the day. It could simply be closing your eyes and taking a couple of deep breaths, or visualizing the synapses in your brain firing as you take in new information. If you sense your mind wandering, perform your ritual to get back on track.

- *Find an organizational method that works for you*: Whether it's writing out a task list or organizing tasks on your phone or tablet or any other method of organization, find one that works for you and stick to it. Refer back to your list or app on a regular basis, especially if you are unsure of what you should be focused on at any point during the day.

- *Change where you work*: Most people doing work that requires mental exertion find that a periodic change in setting helps increase both focus and creativity. Working in the same environment day after day can actually contribute to mental sluggishness. You may want to work outside sometimes, or in a quiet space at the library. Experiment with different settings, and find out what works.

- *Perform focusing exercises*: Like physical conditioning, some people find it helpful to perform focusing exercises. These could be something as simple as counting backward in your head from 100 to 0 by 3s, or something as complicated as a puzzle or math problem.

Remember, mastering your mind is really part of the larger journey to complete self-mastery. This is not something we can expect to attain fully, but rather a skill that we can continually improve. This improvement brings not only greater productivity, but greater well-being. As Cicero said so many centuries ago, "That person then . . . whose mind is quiet through consistency and self-control, who finds contentment in himself, who neither breaks down in adversity nor crumbles in fright, nor burns with any thirsty need nor dissolves into wild and futile excitement, that person is the wise one we are seeking, and that person is happy."[14]

Six

Neuroplasticity for Breakfast

NEUROPLASTICITY REFERS TO OUR brain's ability to change. As we've already discussed, scientists once believed that our brains were essentially done growing and changing when we reached adulthood. But throughout the last several years, rapid advancements in neuroscience have demonstrated that our brains actually produce new neurons until our dying day.[1]

When we are young, our brains contain billions of nerve cells or neurons. As we grow, these neurons branch out and form millions of synapses (connections with other neurons) each day. The connections form networks, and it is these networks of synapses that actually store our knowledge and experiences. The more we use a particular network of neurons, the denser it grows, while the less frequently used networks shrink and may disappear. Quite a bit of this "synaptic pruning" occurs between early childhood and puberty; about half of these synaptic connections will disappear by the time we are adults.[2] The rapid formation of new neural networks and the trimming of disused ones appear to be why children learn so quickly and think so creatively.

The process of forming new neural networks slows down considerably after we reach adulthood, but it does not stop. In his book *The Social Animal*, author David Brooks explains, "With effort, practice, and experience, you can improve the subtlety of your networks. Violinists have dense connections in the area of the brain related to their left hand, because they use it so much while playing their instrument. Once circuits are formed, that increases the chances the same circuits will fire in the future. The neural networks embody our experiences, and in turn guide our future action. The networks of neural connections are the physical manifestation of your habits, personality, and predilections. You are the spiritual entity that emerges out of the material networks in your head."[3]

Just as we continue to form new neural networks in adulthood, our brains continue to trim back the networks we don't use as much. There can be several reasons the adult brain will form a new network or get rid of an old one, including exposure to injury, illness, and stimuli. When the brain is damaged by trauma or disease, not only can new neurons form to begin to replace those that have died, but the brain will also begin to reorganize itself to compensate for the lost capacity.

For example, when people who were previously able to see go blind, the part of their brains associated with vision does not go completely quiet. Instead, the visual cortex begins to fire in response to their fingers when they are reading Braille. This kind of brain "rewiring" can be compared to routing cars through a detour when a particular stretch of roadway is blocked.

We are also learning that the entire nervous system can repair itself after injury far more effectively than previously thought. When Christopher Reeve— known for his portrayal of Superman in the 1970s and 1980s—fell from his horse in 1995, he shattered two cervical vertebrae and was left paralyzed from the neck down. Although his spinal cord was not completely severed, it was severely damaged enough that doctors held out little hope that he would ever regain feeling or movement in his body. Unable to breathe without the help of a respirator, it was a miracle that he even made it to the hospital alive.[4]

Once he recovered enough to be released from the hospital, Reeve continued to act in spite of his paralysis. And he also fought to reverse it, disregarding the grim prognosis he had received from his doctors.

Reeve underwent epidural stimulation, using a special machine to send electrical impulses to stimulate his muscles and encourage his brain to begin sending and receiving information to and from the paralyzed areas of the body. Although he died tragically of cardiac arrest in 2004, doctors continue to make great strides with the treatment he helped to pioneer. Just 10 years after his death, four paralyzed subjects regained the ability to stand and move their legs, as well as bowel and bladder control and sexual function, thanks to epidural stimulation.[5]

We are only just beginning to understand the nervous system's capacity for regeneration and its implications for the treatment of injury and disease. Nerve growth factor (NGF)—a group of proteins produced naturally by the body—is now known to stimulate neuronal sprouting. NGF has been used in experimental treatment of patients with Alzheimer's disease, as well as other forms of dementia, with great promise.[6]

The adult brain, like the juvenile brain, also adapts and grows in response to the stimuli that life throws at us and the stimuli we choose to expose ourselves to. The brain can change in positive ways (such as when we learn a new skill), or in negative ways (such as when someone develops an addiction). Yet few take advantage of this capacity to influence how our brains develop over time.

So how can we effectively leverage our brain's neuroplasticity to become more productive and creative?

There are several different ways to encourage the brain to lay down new neural pathways and trim back others, but they do not work instantaneously. The key is to apply these techniques consistently so that we can maximize the results we want.

Possibility and Belief

Doctors made their prognosis in the case of Christopher Reeve based on all the information they had available at the time. But Reeve's refusal to give up hope was instrumental in his recovery. Multiple studies demonstrate that, in the cases of accidents or even serious illnesses, known medical realities dictate our medical outcomes only to a certain extent; what we believe can happen also plays a very important role in determining our fate. Patients with hope will almost always outlive patients in despair, even if their medical diagnoses are identical.

A colleague of mine, Steve, was struck by a car when he was just 30 years old. After he emerged from a three-week coma, his father elected not to share the details of the doctors' devastating prognosis: that Steve would likely never walk again, would have heavily impaired speech, and should not expect to return to his law practice.

Instead, Steve's father told him that his recovery was going to be long and require a lot of work, but that he was going to be just fine. As we have already discussed, hope and positive anticipation produce an entirely different chemical response in the brain than pain and despair. Three years later, although a lingering speech impediment limited his work to case preparation, Steve was back in the office. Rather than focusing on what he could not control, he excelled at this new role and rose quickly through the ranks of his profession.

Today, Steve leads a thriving and well-respected practice with a national presence. His speech impediment has all but disappeared and he walks with a barely perceptible limp. He credits his remarkable recovery to his hope, optimism, and belief in those crucial early months, a testament to the importance of what we believe is possible.

Does our belief about possibility affect any of the efforts we make to rewire our brains for the sake of improving our creativity and productivity? Dr. Carol Dweck's research (mentioned in Chapter 4) suggests that it does and that the affect is very great. The crux of Dweck's research has been that the belief (or "growth mindset") that abilities—whether they are athletic, intellectual, or artistic—are malleable ("plastic") is extremely important to "adopting learning-oriented behavior."[7]

Dweck knew her findings had revolutionary implications for education, so she developed a program called Brainology that "shows students that they are in control of their brain and its development."[8] The

program teaches students about the process by which their brains lay down new neural networks as they learn. They begin to think of their brains like muscles that will get stronger ("smarter") as they exercise them more and more. As the techniques behind Brainology have been tested, this kind of growth mindset training has been shown not only to boost achievement and motivation, but also to narrow the gender and racial gap in achievement.[9] In 2008, Children and Adults with Attention Deficit/Hyperactivity Disorder (CHADD) recognized Brainology with their Innovative Program of the Year award.

Learning from Athletes

Perhaps one of the clearest demonstrations of the power of neural networks that has been deliberately strengthened is with elite athletes. Athletes regularly complete feats of skill, strength, and speed that seem to defy the known laws of physics, all in the high-pressure environment of competition. As we might expect, their bodies are different from everyone else's: they are stronger, faster, better coordinated, and have longer endurance. But modern neuroscience also reveals that brains of elite athletes function differently from the brains of non-athletes.

Writing in *Discover Magazine*, Carl Zimmer explains the mental component of physical actions: "The brain begins by setting a goal . . . and calculates the best course of action to reach it." For everything from putting on our socks to running a mile, our brains are making calculations about which muscles to contract or relax in order to perform the action best. Zimmer goes on to say, "Athletes may perform better than the rest of us because their brains can find better solutions than ours do." He then cites the research of Claudio

Del Percio of Sapienza University in Rome, who measured brainwaves from athletes and non-athletes, both at rest and in action. Perhaps counterintuitively, Del Percio found that the brains of athletes showed less activity than those of non-athletes, both at rest and while performing physical tasks.[10]

Zimmer writes, "The reason, Del Percio argues, is that the brains of athletes are more efficient, so they produce the desired result with the help of fewer neurons. Del Percio's research suggests that the more efficient a brain, the better job it does in sports. He further explains that when we are learning something new, the part of our brain that controls executive function (the pre-frontal cortex) is very active. After we master an activity, this region becomes much quieter. Del Percio found that this region was very quiet in athletes when they were performing an action well, like hitting the center of a target in pistol shooting.

Commentators for sports such as figure skating and gymnastics will often note that athletes giving superior performances appear to do so effortlessly. This is not because of the athlete's inborn ability (no one is born with the ability to do a triple-axel in ice skates, or a double-layout flip on a mat) but rather because he or she has practiced so much that the execution of the skills has become almost completely automated. They will perform their routine hundreds of times in the weeks leading up to a high-stakes competition to prepare their bodies and their brains to execute perfectly on command.

But physical repetition is just one of the ways in which elite athletes automate their performances. A growing number of athletes in all sports practice visualization or "mental repetitions" of their routines as well. Jack Nicklaus, one of the first professional athletes to talk about visualization, famously said, "I never hit a shot, not even in practice, without having a very sharp, in-focus picture of it in my head. First I see the ball where I want it to finish, nice and white and sitting up high on the bright green grass. Then the scene quickly changes, and I see the ball going there; its path, trajectory, and shape, even its behavior on landing. Then there is a sort of fade-out, and the next scene shows me making the kind of swing that will turn the previous images into reality."[12]

If you watch closely, you will notice football place kickers, basketball players, and tennis players practicing visualization before kicking a field goal, shooting a free throw, or serving a tennis ball. These techniques work because our brains respond very profoundly to images, even when they are generated by our imaginations rather than received by our eyes. When the images (or mental exercises) are selected properly, they can rewire our brains and revolutionize our performance.

In his book *Talent is Overrated: What Really Separates World-Class Performers From Everyone Else*, author Jeffrey Colvin explains that our brains have three "zones" based on the level of challenge we are facing: the comfort zone, the learning zone, and the panic zone. Put a bright sixth grader in an arithmetic class and he may be bored. Put him in a calculus class and he will probably be overwhelmed. But a pre-algebra class may be just the right amount of challenge to maximize his learning.[13]

The key to getting the most out of learning opportunities is what Colvin calls deliberate or "designed" practice. Obviously, we know world-class athletes and musicians do not just log a certain number of hours each week. Their practices are carefully designed by coaches and teachers to allow them to progress through a predetermined course. Often, those practices will be designed to produce a peak performance at a particular competition or match. This same regimen of deliberate practice can be applied to any undertaking—preparing for a presentation, developing a marketing campaign, and so on—but it requires the same cohesive design and expert leadership.

Techniques for Applied Neuroplasticity

The visualization techniques utilized by elite athletes are just one form of applied neuroplasticity. Visualization can also be used to increase both our creativity and our productivity. One of the most important techniques I teach my clients (which I will detail more in Chapter 8) is to begin each day with focused meditation. During this time, I instruct them to visualize in great detail what they hope to accomplish that day as well as each interaction they are likely to have.

This practice serves several purposes. First, it is like a mental dress rehearsal for the day, preparing the brain for the tasks and challenges ahead. Second, it conserves mental energy. This leaves far more brainpower for any creative endeavors or opportunities before you. Think about how different it feels to drive somewhere familiar compared to going somewhere new. Driving on familiar roads allows you to think about other things, carry on a conversation, or listen to an engrossing audiobook. When you are driving somewhere new, you need to focus all your attention on the street signs, exits, and other landmarks. When you take the time to mentally visit your day before it happens, you will have far more brainpower to devote to other tasks.

There are other advantages as well. Rehearsing your day mentally will allow you to pivot more quickly to accommodate any unexpected developments. Furthermore, when you visualize positive outcomes, you flood your brain with the chemicals favorable to bold and creative thinking. Done skillfully, visualizing your goals helps you press through any discouraging developments and overcome any obstacles that may appear during the day.

This type of visualization is actually different from the specific motor-task oriented visualization that athletes practice. In fact, most athletes are taught not to visualize the outcome of the competition, with all its emotional stakes, but rather focus on the motions they must perform as emotionally neutral tasks. Such precise visualization can be helpful if you have a particularly challenging task ahead, such as a job interview or a speech. (We'll talk more about this in Chapter 8.) Morning meditation, rather than training your reflexes or automating specific physical skills, puts you into a bold frame of mind.

It is very important, however, to keep the visualization realistic. It can be tempting to visualize our wildest dreams, but we must not allow our morning meditation to drift into the realm of fantasy. Writing in the *Journal of Experimental Social Psychology*, researchers Heather Kappes and Gabriele Oettingen demonstrated that positive visualization may actually be counterproductive if it is not grounded in reality. As they explain, "Positive fantasies allow people to mentally indulge in a desired future. Whereas previous research found that spontaneously generated positive fantasies about the future predict poor achievement, we examined the effect of experimentally induced positive fantasies about the future. . . . Results indicate that one reason positive fantasies predict poor achievement is because they do not generate energy to pursue the desired future."[14]

In short, the subjects in Kappes and Oettingen's experiments got enough of a dopamine rush from their fantasies to drain their motivation for actual real-life achievements. To be helpful, visualization must focus on the process, not the outcome. Instead of visualizing your company's market share increasing and, as a result, flying around in a private jet, visualize yourself completing your daily tasks in a way that is connected to the growth of that market share. While doing so, anticipate some of the obstacles you may face and consider ways to overcome them. Picture yourself meeting them with confidence and serenity. This way, if you encounter such obstacles you will feel prepared, rather than thrown off course.

It can even be helpful to take a page out of Dweck's Brainology, and visualize your brain forming new synaptic connections while you complete challenging tasks. This can be very helpful when reading a challenging book, working on a particularly difficult problem, or any other task that is intellectually taxing. It can also remind you of the underlying benefit of a duty that is otherwise frustrating.

As you might expect, many of the techniques we discussed in Chapter 3 for encouraging and awakening creativity are also helpful for encouraging your brain's neuroplasticity. Sleep, exercise, a healthy diet, playing a musical instrument, and challenging yourself to try new and difficult things all encourage your brain to lay down new neural networks, strengthen helpful networks, and trim back less efficient connections.

In addition to meditation, immersion techniques for applied neuroplasticity force the brain to reorganize itself more quickly by removing the "easier" option. Our brains are naturally a bit lazy; they conserve energy unless we force them to expend it. There are very good reasons for this. Our prehistoric ancestors needed all the energy they could conserve to run from a predator or capture the night's dinner. But this tendency toward the easiest path runs in opposition to bold, creative thinking.

The most straightforward illustration of an immersion technique is learning a foreign language by traveling to a country in which that language is spoken almost exclusively. You can study Mandarin for years without speaking it or understanding it well. Yet if you spend six months in Beijing living among native speakers, your brain will have no other choice but to become more proficient. You have removed the option of speaking and listening to your native language, which is inherently less work for your brain.

Method actors use a form of immersion when they choose to inhabit the character they are playing for long periods of time. They do this to connect in a deeper way with that character's motivations and emotions. Although not the only way to achieve a good performance, such practices demonstrate the power of immersion to help us actually feel and think differently.

Intense conditioning can also cause the brain to rewire itself in a relatively short period of time. For example, the United States Marine Corps Recruit Training, more commonly known as "boot camp," takes recruits through a grueling 13-week program of physical and mental challenges. Those who emerge from the experience successfully are permanently changed. Not only are they prepared both physically and mentally to face the challenges they are likely to encounter as they serve, but they often have different posture, habits, and attitudes in their daily lives. This kind of conditioning is also utilized in treatment centers for substance abuse or compulsive behaviors. In order to help patients overcome behavior patterns that have become so deeply ingrained, they are brought into a completely new environment and given an entirely new routine.

Applied neuroplasticity can also utilize the properties of mirror neurons to aid mental growth and learning. Ever since mirror neuron theory was developed more than two decades ago (as a result of monkey studies performed at the University of Parma), it has been the subject of much debate and controversy. Some have hailed mirror neurons as holding the secret of what it means to be human, while others have dismissed them as hype.

What we do know is that when we watch someone perform a task, the corresponding areas of our brain light up, just not quite as intensely as if we were performing the activity ourselves. This is nothing new: We've all experienced sympathy pain when we see someone get injured, or a warm rush of emotion when we see two lovers reunited in a movie. We've also watched countless babies and toddlers imitate their parents and older siblings, and we intuitively understand that this is an integral part of how they learn.

There are two immediate takeaways from what we do know about mirror neurons. First, our brains and behavior are influenced by those around us. Athletes will improve more by competing against and training with people of a higher ability level. Musicians who play with others who are at a higher ability level will experience greater improvement as well. The same is true of intellectual and creative endeavors. When you spend meaningful time with those whose abilities exceed your own, you find yourself challenged and stretched.

Second, as David Brooks puts it, "Minds are intensely permeable. Loops exist between brains. The same thought and feeling can arise in different minds, with invisible networks filling the space between them."[15] Mirror neurons remain somewhat mysterious, but they beg the question: which minds are you networking with?

Finding Your Balance

If you have read this far in this book, you are likely a highly driven and dynamic individual. I understand;

I am too, and so are almost all the people I coach. But all of us need balance in our lives. We cannot be constantly immersed in ambition and the drive to succeed. Unmitigated obsession with accomplishment has caused many otherwise brilliant individuals to look back on their lives with deep regrets.

Such behavior also leads to mental and physical burnout. When we rise early and work until the wee hours of the morning day in and day out, we ignore the need of our brains and bodies for high-quality rest, and ultimately sap our creative power. Sleep provides vital support not only for physical health, but also for learning and memory. In a way, sleep helps solidify the changes we make to our brains through applied neuroplasticity.

Researchers Bjorn Rasch and Jan Born write, "Newer findings characterize sleep as a brain state optimizing memory consolidation, in opposition to the waking brain being optimized for encoding of memories. Consolidation originates from reactivation of recently encoded neuronal memory representations, which occur during SWS (Slow Wave Sleep) and transform respective representations for integration into long-term memory."[16] Without good sleep, we will fail to make the most of all the work we do while we are awake.

Most doctors agree that good sleep habits are vital to obtaining high-quality sleep each night and ensuring maximum daytime alertness and productivity. If you take a long time to fall asleep, wake often during the night, or snore frequently, you may need to reevaluate your sleep hygiene. Good habits include common-sense ideas such as avoiding caffeine, alcohol, and food right before bed and waking at the same time each day. Most sleep specialists agree that it is not a good idea to watch television or work in bed, so that you will associate your bed with relaxation and sleep. Exposure to natural light during the day and getting adequate exercise also contribute to good sleep hygiene.

If you snore excessively or if you or your partner think your breathing may be stopping during the night, you should be evaluated for sleep apnea. This is a serious condition that is a major undiagnosed cause of mental sluggishness during the day. It also puts tremendous strain on your heart and can be fatal if left untreated.

Lastly, most people benefit from some sort of bedtime ritual, even if it is fairly simple and short. To ensure high-quality rest, we want to be in the right frame of mind before we sleep. One of the best ways to accomplish this is by taking the time to meditate on all the things you are grateful for before you go to sleep. As we have already mentioned, gratitude provides a natural counterweight to our ambition and goals by reminding us of what we already have. A 2009 study published in the *Journal of Psychosomatic Research* found that individuals who expressed gratitude experienced higher-quality sleep than those who didn't.[17]

Often we receive innovative ideas and inspiring thoughts during our sleep. We may wake in the morning with an idea that we will forget if we don't write it down immediately. Keep a pad of paper or a tablet by the bedside so that you can record any of these spontaneous inspirations.

Waking refreshed and energized is a sign that both your body and your brain have gotten what they need from their time asleep. This is the best possible way to prepare for a productive and creative day. Expect a lot from your brain during the day, but reward it with good sleep each night.

We've just scratched the surface of our brains' potential for growth, even in adulthood. Science continues to reveal in even greater detail the ways in which our neural networks can change and develop throughout our lives. In the next chapter, we'll explore how to orchestrate these new connections in a way that revolutionizes how we think and perform.

Seven

Disrupting Your Mind ... Rearranging Reality

WHEN ALBERT EINSTEIN PUBLISHED his general theory of relativity a century ago, even he could not have foreseen how drastically it would change the world. Einstein did not claim to discover a new species of moth nor was he offering a new theory about the cause of the dinosaurs' extinction; he was proposing a radically different view of reality as it was understood at the time.

Although most of us think of quantum physics as unfathomably abstract, Einstein's theory actually affects our lives on a daily basis. Without it, the Global Positioning System (GPS) navigation devices that are now nearly ubiquitous on smartphones across the world would not be possible. The incredibly precise information relayed by satellites depends on atom clocks, whose ticks are accurate to 20 nanoseconds, according to research by Richard Gray and Alexandra Genova: "Because the satellites are constantly moving relative to the Earth, effects predicted by Einstein's theory must be taken into account . . . . The precision of atomic clocks makes the desired accuracy achievable and GPS technology corrects this discrepancy to make the location accurate."[1]

Change Perception, Change Reality?

Einstein and other quantum physics pioneers did not simply throw out the work of the scientists who had gone before them. Instead they were able to perceive hints that there were phenomena in the universe that Newtonian physics couldn't completely explain. This perception led to curiosity, which in turn led to greater investigation. Their investigations then enabled others to be able to perceive this "new" reality as well.

Our brains are often compared to computers, taking in countless data points through our senses in order to perceive the world around us. This analogy holds true to a point; in actuality, our brains are far more complicated than our laptops. They take in information, but they also interpret it quickly, to enable us to make sense of our surroundings and know how to respond to them. For example, our brains don't just judge the size and speed of an object approaching us; they interpret the information immediately and determine whether or not that object is a threat. In nanoseconds, they tell our bodies whether we should duck to avoid it or reach out to catch it.

But not everyone perceives the same stimuli the same way. We've all heard great athletes speak about how their perception of their surroundings changes when they are performing at their peak. Basketball players report the net appearing wider when they are "in the zone," while baseball players describe the ball as appearing larger when they are hitting well. While such testimonies tend to sound emotional or meta-phorical, an experiment by two Perdue University psychologists demonstrated that there is actually more to it than that.

Researchers asked participants to look at a field goal upright from the 10-yard line and then estimate the width and height of the uprights and crossbar using a scale model. They then gave the subjects 10 attempts to actually kick a field goal. After the last kick participants were asked to estimate the width and height again, using the same model.

All participants estimated the size of the goal equally before they kicked. But those who kicked well consistently estimated the goal posts to be further apart and the crossbar to be lower than those who had kicked poorly.[2] In just a few minutes, their performance had actually altered their perception of reality.

As far as your brain is concerned, you don't have to move mountains in order to rearrange reality. You simply have to find ways to alter your perception. In his book *The As If Principle: The Radically New Approach to Changing Your Life*, author Richard Wiseman cites decades of research that support the idea that our emotions and perceptions actually follow our behavior more than the other way around. For example, choosing to smile can actually cause you to feel happier, while frowning can make you feel worse.[3]

Wiseman also cites the work of Angela Leung at Singapore Management University who conducted two experiments that directly link behavior and creative output. In one experiment, participants were divided into two groups: one stood inside 5-foot square boxes, while the second stood outside. In the other experiment, the first group walked in straight lines, while the second group walked around randomly.

In both experiments participants were then asked to complete some tasks that involved creativity. The people who had been standing outside the boxes or walking randomly demonstrated significantly more creativity than those who had been inside the box or walking in straight lines. As Wiseman observes, "Behaving in a creative way directly influenced the way the participants thought."[4]

Keys to Disruptive Thinking

Among contemporary disruptive thinkers, it is difficult to find anyone more remarkable than Martine Rothblatt. Rothblatt is a lawyer by training, as well as a pianist, triathlete, and world traveler, among other things. She not only invented satellite radio, but also started a biotechnology firm that produced a lifesaving medication to treat her daughter's lung condition, which was considered terminal at the time of diagnosis.

Rothblatt's "first creation" of satellite radio occurred in the 1980s. While taking a break from UCLA, she lived for a time on the Seychelles Islands off the coast of Kenya. "While there, a buddy took Rothblatt to a U.S. satellite installation. There—right *there*—is where she says her mind took an exponential leap forward, imagining how close future worlds really were."[5]

It took almost two decades before this revelation was converted into the launch of a national satellite radio service. In 1990, Rothblatt founded Satellite CD Radio and began petitioning the FCC for permission to obtain unused satellite frequencies for radio-like broadcasts. The benefits she promised included static-free transmissions that would reach all over the world instead of just the perimeter of an FM or AM station. However, there were just a few glitches to work out of the business plan. As the *New York Times* reported in 1992, "But [satellite radio] listeners will first have to buy entirely new radios, which do not yet exist. And the market for the new services remains unclear. So it is not certain when, or if, satellite radio stations will go on the air."[6]

But they did. Once the regulatory barriers were cleared, the company merged with its largest competitor and today serves tens of millions of customers worldwide as Sirius XM Radio. Perhaps ironically, by the time this success had been achieved, Rothblatt had moved on to an entirely different endeavor. Motivated by her daughter's severe and rare illness, Rothblatt founded United Therapeutics in 1996. In just a few years she had successfully brought an orphan drug (a drug that treats a rare condition) to market and saved her daughter's life, along with the lives of about 30,000 individuals suffering from the same condition. Rothblatt successfully revolutionized the way drug therapies are developed just as she had affected ways that people listen to radio programs.

Since the initial success of United Therapeutics, Rothblatt is pioneering new ways to increase the number of human lungs that are can be transplanted into needy recipients. She is even raising genetically modified pigs in order to utilize their organs for human transplant. So what does this remarkable woman have to say about creating such disruptive innovations?

Rothblatt sums up what she believes are the most important components of the creative process: be curious, question authority, act lovingly, and do practically.[7] Authentic curiosity is essential to creativity and disruptive thinking. Only when we are truly curious what will be able to not just question the status quo, but actually alter it.

Author Elizabeth Gilbert encourages people to follow their curiosity rather than their passion when seeking out a life calling. As she told *New York Magazine*, "Passion burns hot and fast, which means it can come and go. Curiosity is so accessible and available . . . most of the time, when you're stuck, you can think, *Is it possible that you can't find one little tiny thing in the world that is interesting to you?*"[8]

Questioning authority is frequently misunderstood as having contempt for authority or treating those in authority with disrespect. However, Rothblatt and others like her simply question the assumptions that those in charge are making. Satellite radio had multitudes of detractors in the early days, from traditional radio stations that did not welcome competition to critics who assumed it would be impossible to develop an entirely new market for the service. Similarly, pharmaceutical companies assumed that there was no way to make money on a drug for a condition as rare as the one that afflicted her daughter. Rothblatt didn't rage against these authorities; she simply rearranged reality and proved them wrong.

It is obvious how Rothblatt acted lovingly in all the remarkable things she achieved. Even the techniques she is working on to improve the transplant rate for donated lungs are developed with the understanding that her daughter may one day need a lung transplant. What purer motivation for innovation can there be than saving the life of a child? Yet we can all access that same love by working to innovate for the good of humanity, even if that innovation merely improves a product or makes part of the production process more efficient.

Although she is clearly a phenomenally big thinker, Rothblatt has always labored in the practical realm, working tirelessly to translate first creation into second creation. Far from limiting her imagination, her practical experiments have led to mind-blowing ideas for the future that have earned admiration from some of the world's leading innovators. Such futuristic possibilities include robots that may be uploaded with a person's memories and experiences, in such a way that it can continue to share them with future generations.[9] In that way, Rothblatt says, the owner of the robot can outlive his or her body. (Is that disruptive enough for you?)

Disrupting the Status Quo

So how, on a practical level, do we disrupt our minds so that we can move closer to this kind of disruptive thinking? We've talked about a lot of lifestyle adjustments to cultivate creativity, raising our levels of dopamine and lowering the levels of stress hormones like cortisol. But what can we do during the creative process to help our brains question assumptions and avoid doing what we have always done?

Changing the way the brain functions is not always a good thing. Concussions and other traumatic brain injuries, drug abuse, and disease can all alter the brain in a negative way. For centuries, people experimented with hallucinogenic drugs to escape reality or to try to obtain various kinds of enlightenment. And not so long ago people like Ram Dass and Timothy Leary advocated such experimentation in order to reach a higher level of consciousness.

Of course there are some medical reasons to take radical steps to deliberately alter brain function. Some people's brains are stuck in deep depression, post-traumatic stress disorder, or in patterns of drug or alcohol abuse. Electroconvulsive therapy (ECT)—often referred to as electroshock therapy—works by sending small pulses of electricity through the brain, triggering short seizures. Other therapies utilize magnetic pulses on the surface of the head for the same purpose.

Deep Brain Stimulation (DBS) is another method for treating Parkinson's disease, obsessive compulsive disorder, and depression. During DBS, a pacemaker-like device is surgically implanted under the collarbone and electrodes are placed onto different regions of the brain, depending on the disorder being treated. The device emits a regular pulse of electricity, which seems to "reset" the malfunctioning region of the brain.

Obviously, such therapies carry varying degrees of risk and are undertaken only in fairly extreme circumstances. Cognitive behavior therapy (CBT) is a much lower-risk intervention. It is used in many milder cases, and its remarkable success rate has much to teach us about the safe, deliberate disruption and alteration of brain function. CBT is a non-surgical, non-chemical approach to "rewiring" the brain that has proven remarkably effective in treating anxiety, depression, other mental illnesses, and even some chronic pain disorders.[10]

As we discussed in Chapter 3, certain experiences trigger thoughts in our brains, which in turn trigger a chemical response. If we see a beautiful flower, smell a delicious meal, or feel an embrace from a good friend, we experience positive thoughts, which in turn flood our brain with dopamine, serotonin, and so on. When a threatening stimulus provokes negative thoughts, the chemical response includes stress hormones like cortisol. In some people, this negative feedback loop becomes so prominent that everyday experiences can trigger a disproportionate stress response, and the brain becomes almost permanently flooded with the wrong chemicals.

CBT enables individuals to intervene in this cycle, teaching them to respond to the experience or stimulus with positive, more accurate thoughts. This prevents the negative chemical response and breaks the cycle. Studies in the use of CBT with post-traumatic stress disorder (PTSD) have strongly suggested that CBT exercises actually make physiological changes in the brain. A study at the National Institute of Psychiatry and Addictions at the University of Szeged (Hungary) took MRIs of the brains of trauma victims before and after CBT treatment, as well as collecting blood samples to analyze the levels of stress hormones. After therapy, victims showed a higher volume in the area of the brain (the hippocampus) that regulates emotion and lower levels of stress hormones.

Lead researcher Dr. Szabolcs Kéri explained that these results showed "structural changes in the brain, such as the shrinkage of the hippocampus, are reversible in trauma victims. [CBT] may help normalize these alterations and improve symptoms ... the regeneration of hippocampus correlated with the expression of a gene that balances the activity of the stress hormone cortisol . . ."[11]

Techniques for Disruptive Thinking

So we now know that the brain is malleable, and with techniques like CBT, we can intentionally rearrange our brain's reality to address mental illness, depression, and anxiety. But what are the best ways to rearrange reality in healthy brains for the sake of increasing creativity and productivity? There are several different techniques, which I have used to coach both individuals and groups successfully. Different models may work better for different individuals, different companies, and even for different problems.

Before utilizing any of these techniques, I always help my clients clearly define the problem they are trying to tackle and the objectives they hope to achieve with their creative endeavors. Then, depending on their goals, needs, and preferences, we may try any of the following.

Synectics

George Prince and William J.J. Gordon created synectics in the 1960s, although it has been underutilized in the years since. They developed the technique after analyzing thousands of hours of audio tapes recorded during product development meetings. They listened and took notes with the goal of determining why some meetings were so much more fruitful than others. The two concluded that the difference wasn't necessarily who was in the room, but rather how the meeting was led and the nature of the interaction between the meeting participants.

Writing about the method in the *Harvard Business Review* in 1969, Prince explained four major stumbling blocks for the leader of an innovative meeting: 1) He noted that even meetings with a clear agenda may not have a clear objective. Just because everyone knows the items that will be covered in the meeting doesn't mean they all understand the larger purpose;

2) leaders often unintentionally discourage creativity, even during meetings that are supposed to solve problems; 3) leaders often use their power to discourage dissent; and 4) most people's natural reaction in meetings is to be antagonistic to new ideas. As a result of these stumbling blocks, leaders often conclude that it is difficult to get any good ideas out of meetings.

The solution Prince proposed was to change the dynamics of the meeting by applying a different technique as a leader. He explained, "Our experiments with creative group leadership make it clear that the chairman *can* multiply the effectiveness of his people." But to do this, Prince said, the leader must think differently. "He must come to view himself as the servant of the group . . . and as such he must devote his entire attention to helping the group use its wits."[12]

Prince and Gordon's synectics techniques further work to disrupt the typical flow of such meetings, and allow participants to interact in new and unexpected ways. Because of all the previously mentioned stumbling blocks, it is sometimes helpful to have an external facilitator who is not part of the organization's formal leadership structure to lead such meetings. However, the techniques can be applied effectively by anyone with the right training.

I have successfully coached many groups through synectics exercises, which have enabled them to produce meaningful innovations and solutions. The session starts with the group selecting an object out of a box, which could be anything from a coffee grinder, to an umbrella, to a tennis ball. The group then lists 45 qualities of the object: 15 characteristics, 15 potential uses, and 15 things that the object might say or feel. For example, if your group selected a tennis ball, it might be described as round, green, fuzzy (and 12 other adjectives). It could be used for playing tennis, juggling, or massaging sore muscles, and if it could talk, it might say it wanted to be played with more, and so on.

These exercises are completed very quickly, and then the group is asked to associate the answers to the questions with the task or problem before them, whether it is developing a new product or service, a new marketing campaign, or any other kind of innovation. To associate the tennis ball with the product or campaign they were addressing, the group might ask, "What would a round solution look like? What would a green solution look like?"

Time and time again, this technique has yielded some incredible solutions for companies I have coached, including rebranding a major consumer goods product for an international marketing campaign. The process will reliably produce ideas that would never have come up otherwise. Of course the reason it works is not because a tennis ball holds any particular relationship to the product; instead the exercise stirs up the creativity of the group. By forcing the mind to associate two objects or ideas that appear to be completely unrelated, the brain is forced to form new connections and ignore old ones. Because everyone is doing it together, people become less resistant to change and more open to new ideas.

The study of random objects by focusing on their nature, their function, and their fictional "souls" also forces us into the mindset of a creator. Creation is always undertaken with these qualities, which are both infinitely abstract and deeply practical, in mind. When we create something, we give it a nature, a function, and in a way we put a little piece of our own soul into it. True creators love their creations, even as they are motivated by love to create.

When NASA sent two rovers, Spirit and Opportunity, to explore Mars in January 2004, they immediately began transmitting data about their new planet back to their creators on Earth. Among the many important pieces of information they uncovered was evidence that Mars likely contained water billions of years ago. When the rovers finally stopped functioning years later, their creators felt genuine sadness.

"We have developed a strong emotional attachment to both of these rovers. They are just the cutest darn things out in the solar system. . . . They are beautiful, accomplished little proxies out on the surface of Mars and we're quite proud of them and have become quite attached to them," project manager John Callas explained.[13]

Lastly, synectics works because it's fun. It doesn't take long, so people don't worry about wasting time. It releases dopamine in the brain and encourages everyone to think a little differently than they normally would, and ultimately brings the best out of all present.

The Case Study

In many fields, professionals are encouraged to practice their craft in hypothetical situations. Lawyers participate in mock-trials, doctors respond to fictional patient symptoms often taken from past cases, and first responders participate in drills for various kinds of disasters. Such exercises offer participants a chance to develop their skills in low-risk environments, so that when the real situation arises, they are better prepared.

The same kinds of case studies can be very valuable for innovative leaders. Not long ago I was leading a session at a university that was hosting a conference on innovation. We divided the attendees into groups and gave them each real-life marketing scenarios that major companies had to deal with in the past. These challenges included Coca Cola's 2001 decision—as Africa's largest private employer—to join the fight against HIV/AIDS by utilizing its advertising network. Another favorite was MTV's 2007 push to penetrate the Middle Eastern market with its programming, despite their very different values and standards of what is acceptable to show on television.

Each group had to draft proposals of how they would meet the unique challenges offered by each scenario and then present them to the group. In a surprising number of cases, the students came up with innovations and solutions that were very similar to the ones that the actual companies had employed. In others, they came up with ideas that were even more creative than what was actually done to solve the problem.

Such exercises have great value because they offer students and professionals the chance to gain experience and build confidence. They begin the exercise knowing that the company successfully overcame the challenge, so no matter how difficult it seems, they know it is possible. When they are finished they are much better prepared to tackle whatever real-life challenge they are presented with.

Sarcasm and Creativity

Oscar Wilde famously quipped that sarcasm was the lowest form of wit but the highest form of intelligence. Although many use sarcasm as a defense mechanism to avoid being open or vulnerable with their colleagues, it can also be a surprisingly effective catalyst for creativity. According to a study published in *Organizational Behavior and Human Decision Processes*, participants demonstrated three times the creative problem-solving ability after hearing a sarcastic message compared to a sincere one.[14]

To understand how to use sarcasm to trigger creativity in oneself and others, it is important to steer clear of angry, insulting, or defensive sarcasm. For example, responding to constructive criticism of an idea with a sarcastic compliment to the speaker will only instigate conflict. But within trusting relationships there is a playful form of sarcasm that can have quite the opposite effect. For many years in my own executive coaching, I have used playful sarcasm both to break the ice in high-pressure situations and stimulate creative thinking in individuals as well as groups of people.

Researchers investigating the positive effect of sarcastic remarks on creativity note that sarcasm requires the brain to think abstractly, because the plain meaning of the statement is different from its actual meaning. As several researchers note, "Sarcasm often makes salient contradictory notions. As a result, both constructing and making sense of any type of sarcasm necessitate recognizing and reconciling disparate ideas, making sarcasm a potential facilitator of creativity on both sides of the exchange."[15] In other words, both giving and receiving sarcasm forces your brain to think in a way that is more conducive to creativity.

Arts-Based Activities

According to a 2005 study, arts-based activities such as improvisational theater, drawing and music help stimulate creativity in a business context. The findings indicated that "arts-based activities can be effective as a vehicle for showcasing, enhancing, and/or stimulating creativity in executive leaders."[16] Although getting a bunch of business professionals together to paint or play the piano might seem like a passing fad, more and more companies are trying it.

Remember: The goal of such activities isn't to become a better artist or musician, it's to stimulate creativity by disrupting the brain's normal thinking process. Large companies, including innovation giants like Google, are sending their executives and employees to participate in improvisational theater training sessions.[17] Initially touted as a communication tool to help more reserved employees come out of their shells, a growing number of companies are finding it is a useful tool to help improve the creative dynamic of their teams.

Just like in a real performance, participants in an improv session take a suggestion from the audience and create a scene together as they go along. This not only improves communication and creativity, but also adaptability and the willingness to take risk. Perfectionism, although fine when one is in the process of proofing the final copy of a brochure, can murder the creative process. Improv can help people gain the confidence to share their ideas, even if they seem off the wall or aren't yet fully developed. As improvisational instructor Rick Andrews explains, "If people aren't confident, they don't contribute as much, so you lose. It's like group writers' block: You only toss your idea out there if it's perfect."[18]

I have personally led groups in carefully directed theater games that even involved props and costumes. We have taken retreats for a few days, clearly defined the problem we were trying to solve, and used theater games to share the ideas and vision of the solution. Sometimes participants will even create a video, which employs other creative activities like editing and sound engineering. Again, the goal is not to master these tasks; it's to disrupt conventional thinking and awaken creativity.

You don't need to do anything drastic to disrupt your mind and rearrange reality. You just need to be open about doing something a little out of the ordinary. In the next chapter, we'll examine more techniques that will help you realize both your short-term and long-term goals.

Eight

Bold Visions and Powerful Strategies

How can you go from being a creative individual to a leader of a creative powerhouse? Up to this point, we have focused on the neuroscience behind creativity, the logistics of the creative process itself, and various techniques to enhance imagination and ultimately innovation. Now we will examine the challenge of creating a compelling, bold vision that will inspire and unify others in the pursuit of innovation and ingenuity.

Of course leading an innovative organization requires many of the same skills needed to lead any organization effectively. Creative leaders must have strong listening and communication skills and the ability to connect meaningfully with all different kinds of people. They must be good problem-solvers and decision-makers, and they must be able to manage time, money, and a wide variety of tasks effectively. Whenever possible, they should lead with influence instead of wielding their authority.

But the leaders of bold, innovative organizations have an even greater challenge. They must chart a clear course through all the risks and unknown factors associated with uncharted territory. They must bring out the best in each of their people without burning anyone out. Ultimately, they must create a sense of stability in the midst of disruptive change while creating a sense of unity among what is often a very diverse group of individuals.

Limiting Beliefs

We have already alluded to limiting beliefs: the subconscious, often unexamined assumptions we make about life and ourselves that prevent us from reaching our full potential. Leaders of innovative organizations must effectively identify and deal with these beliefs not only in themselves, but also in the individuals they lead.

But limiting beliefs affect us beyond an individual level. They also affect groups of people and their interactions with each other. Families, communities, companies, and entire nations can have their culture and performance negatively influenced by these beliefs, making it even more important to eliminate them effectively.

Fear of Failure

As we discussed in Chapter 4, failure is an inevitable part of innovation, and how we respond to failure greatly influences how much momentum we are able to generate during the creative process. The fear of failure is perhaps one of the most common but also one of the most toxic factors that cause us to unknowingly sabotage our own performance. The fear of failure is completely opposed to bold, decisive action, making us averse to any kind of risk. Furthermore, leadership driven by such fear can never inspire others to follow wholeheartedly.

Yet not everyone who suffers from the fear of failure is aware of the problem. We often do not consciously realize that we are being driven by an irrational worry that we will not succeed, and that our lack of success will have catastrophic consequences. Some signs that the fear of failure may be lurking just beneath the surface include physical symptoms such as stomach aches or headaches, especially before an important meeting or presentation. The fear of failure can also show up as a resistance to trying new things or procrastinating when an important deadline is looming.

In a group context, the fear of failure can make an entire department or even a whole company resistant to new ideas or innovations. It can cause people to undermine change even when it is obvious that the company is on the brink of going out of business by shifts in the market or in the economy. And as we have already discussed, fear of failure is exacerbated by corporate cultures that demand instant success and are unwilling to allow new products or services enough time to succeed.

Fear of Rejection

Many fears, whether it is a fear of public speaking or a fear of intimacy, often boil down to a fear of rejection. Human beings are social creatures, and we are wired to belong to a group. Even deeply introverted people— those who gain energy from being by themselves— have the need to connect meaningfully with others. On an emotional level, rejection tells us that we are unlovable or unworthy. Although the fear of rejection is a deeply personal and individual fear, it can affect our performance at work, our ability to be creative, and certainly our ability to lead.

Many people deal with the fear of rejection by refusing to be open, honest, and vulnerable. Naturally, this is toxic to personal relationships, but it is also greatly damaging to creative endeavors. After all, sharing new ideas makes us vulnerable, and sometimes it is easy to interpret the rejection of one of our ideas, by other people or by the market, as a rejection of ourselves as human beings.

Egotistical behavior such as bullying is almost always a mask for the fear of rejection. This is because those who are desperately afraid that others will not approve of them will often try to reject others first. Most egotistical leaders will never succeed in leading a truly innovative organization, because their desire for personal fame or glory prevents them from bringing out the best in others (who could potentially pass them by and then reject them afterward).

When the fear of rejection dominates a group, people are usually reluctant or unwilling to share new ideas. Individuals or even entire departments may work to undermine each other instead of supporting one another's efforts. This may be especially true during time periods when the organization is forced to make cuts in either salaries or jobs. People may become more committed to preserving the budget of their department than the overall good of the company.

Fear of the Future

We are born into a world of uncertainty. When we have loving relationships and a stable environment, we tend to look toward the future with hope and expectation. When these things are not present, we tend to look forward with apprehension, frustration, and even fear. Regardless of how much of the world is out of our control (more on this in the next chapter), humans have a deep need to feel like we have some degree of self-determination.

Self Determination Theory (SDT), a theory of motivation developed by Edward L. Deci and Richard M. Ryan, further explains and analyzes this need: "Conditions supporting the individual's experience of autonomy, competence, and relatedness are argued to foster the most volitional and high quality forms of motivation and engagement for activities, including enhanced performance, persistence, and creativity. In addition SDT proposes that the degree to which any of these three psychological needs is unsupported or thwarted within a social context will have a robust detrimental impact on wellness in that setting."[1]

People respond to feeling a lack of autonomy, competence, or relatedness in a variety ways, few of them helpful. Some may adopt a fatalistic attitude, resigning themselves to a philosophy of "whatever happens, happens." These individuals will often stop making any effort to achieve their goals or improve their lives, focusing instead on short-term pleasures. Others will seek an unreasonable amount of power over the things they feel they can control. In extreme cases those with this outlook on life may fall into substance abuse in an effort to alleviate their emotional suffering.

In a group context, the fear of the future shows up in the form of apathy and disengagement, as well as in hyper-controlling behavior. Controlling individuals may micromanage those who report to them, or seek to control a project they are not actually supposed to lead. Naturally such behavior discourages creativity and suppresses innovation.

Addressing Limiting Beliefs

The problem with all of these limiting beliefs is that simply knowing that they are unhelpful and even inaccurate is often not enough to prevent them from shaping the way we think and behave. Particularly when such beliefs have been entrenched in an individual or a group for a significant period of time, it can take a great deal of time and effort to excise them and replace them with more helpful, accurate ideas. Yet for thousands of years, many people have done just that through prayer and meditation.

Meditation, once dismissed as the territory of mystics and hippies, has now been studied extensively and found to have measurable, positive effects on practitioners' brains and overall sense of well-being. It is not a magic pill, but rather a practice that takes consistent effort over a period of time. That said, almost anyone can learn to meditate, and belief in a particular religion or philosophy is not necessary to benefit from its practice.

Harvard neuroscientist Sara Lazar studied brain scans of long-term meditators compared to those of a control group of non-meditators. She found that the meditators had more gray matter in the insula and sensory regions. In an interview with the *Washington Post*, she explained further, "We also found they had more gray matter in the frontal cortex, which is associated with working memory and executive decision making. It's well-documented that our cortex shrinks as we get older . . . in this one region of the prefrontal cortex, 50-year-old meditators had the same amount of gray matter as 25-year-olds."[2] In short, meditation helps to keep the brain young.

But you do not have to meditate for years to see benefits. Another study Lazar conducted examined the effects of an eight-week meditation program conducted with people who had never meditated before compared to a control group. The group that learned meditation showed an increase in volume in four different regions of the brain, which controlled things like learning, cognition, memory, emotional regulation and perspective.[3] A UC Santa Barbara study also demonstrated that meditation training reduced mind-wandering and increased performance on the GRE exam.[4]

Types of Meditation

There are countless forms of meditation, but most fall into one of three major categories: controlled focus, open monitoring, and self-transcending.[5]

- *Controlled focus:* Zen is one of the more famous forms of controlled focus meditation that dates back centuries to Japanese Buddhism. Zen is often performed sitting down in a group with an instructor who guides students. Practitioners are taught to focus on a single thing—often the breath or a koan ("riddle")—to empty the mind of distractions and increase one's sense of peace.

- *Open monitoring:* Mindfulness-based meditation employs open monitoring, as discussed in Chapter 5. Practitioners learn to distance themselves from their bodies and minds and dispassionately observe their breath, heartbeat, emotions, and so on.

- *Self-transcending:* Transcendental Meditation (TM) is a form of self-transcending meditation that was developed by the late Maharishi Mahesh Yogi, who drew on thousands of years of Hindu tradition. The technique was made popular during his world tours of the 1950s and 1960s and gained many celebrity devotees, including the Beatles. TM is a mantra-based meditation, involving internal chanting directed by an instructor.

Bob Roth, CEO of the David Lynch Foundation, which provides TM instruction to veterans and abuse survivors, explains the difference between TM and other forms of meditation, which utilize controlled focus or open monitoring: "With TM, you're given a mantra—a word with no meaning—and taught how to use it. The active thinking mind settles down to a state of inner calm without any effort . . . . TM uses sounds or mantra that has no meaning as a vehicle to experience a quieter, less agitated thought process."[6]

Prayer

Billions of humans throughout history have prayed to God (or multiple gods) for various reasons and in various ways. Some have made offerings in front of images or statues, while others have offered silent reverence. Regardless of the particular faith or tradition, almost all prayer contains the elements of thanksgiving and supplication, while many also contain the components of adoration, worship, confession, and repentance.

Although true materialist skeptics will likely find such practices unnecessary or pointless, all kinds of people find it comforting to acknowledge their imperfections and how small they are in comparison to all that exists. Many nonreligious individuals also find prayer a helpful practice, asking the universe or "life" for help rather than a specific deity. They may visualize themselves sending out love to the universe, finding peace with their fellow man, and then asking the universe for what they need.

Prayer acknowledges our human need for moral clarity, a higher purpose in life and connection to something larger than ourselves. Some of us are taught this through our childhood faiths; others may experience it for the first time when they fall in love or have children. For many, regular prayer is a way of remembering what is truly important in life.

Applied Meditation and Prayer

Countless different models exist to apply prayer and meditation to personal and professional goals. For many years, I benefitted greatly from a morning meditation ritual based on the visualization techniques described in Chapter 6. I would visualize myself in my room, and then rising above my house. Gradually, I would see myself rising higher until I would see my entire street, then my town, then the Florida peninsula. As I continued to rise higher, I would see the entire globe, solar system, the Milky Way, and at last the universe. From that point, outside space and time, I would begin to visualize myself having success at each task and interaction I anticipated for the day ahead.

Several things would happen to me during this time. I would experience the emotions associated with success: excitement, happiness, and peace. I would also see myself taking all the small steps needed to make that success happen: paying attention to detail, expending focused, effective effort, connecting well with others, and being generous and kind.

When I was finished visualizing my day, I would "return" by coming back to our galaxy, solar system, planet, country, and finally to my neighborhood, home, and room. I personally found that my days went much better when I took the time to do this meditation than when I didn't, and many of the individuals I have coached had the same experience.

Another approach to personal and professional development, Neuro-linguistic Programming (NLP), was founded by Richard Bandler and John Grinder during the 1970s and remains popular in the business world today. According to the Association for Neuro-Linguistic Programing, "NLP is frequently known as the 'user's manual for your mind,' . . . it looks at the way in which we think and process our thoughts (Neuro), the language patterns we use (Linguistic) and our behaviors (Programming), and how these interact to have a positive (or negative) effect on us as individuals."[7] We will cover one particularly powerful type of guided NLP technique, Neurological Level Alignment, in the next chapter.

The Time Machine Experience

One of the biggest leadership challenges in an innovation-driven industry is motivating and empowering groups of people to sustain creative and disruptive thinking during a long period of time. The prayer and meditation techniques we have discussed so far are designed to help individuals reduce stress, increase focus, or reach any number of personal or professional goals. Even when meditation is taught and practiced in a group setting, the objective is typically to help all the people in the group pursue their individual aims.

Taking many principles from properly applied NLP, I have developed what I call the Time Machine Experience. It effectively harnesses the power of both visualization and other NLP techniques, and allows them to be applied in a group context for the purpose of achieving a collective rather than an individual goal. The Time Machine Experience can be used when a company would like to develop a bold vision and strategy, or is at a crossroads or facing a crisis. It can also be used proactively in anticipation of shifts in the market or in the economy. In fact, I believe any group with a collective purpose—whether it is a nonprofit organization, an educational entity, or even a family— can find great value in the exercise at any time in their growth and development. There are four major steps in the Time Machine exercise.

Preparation

During the preparation phase, I encourage partici- pants to begin to let go of their fears and any negative assumptions they may be making about the future.

I particularly encourage them to stop thinking in terms of probabilities ("What is likely to happen?") and start thinking in terms of possibilities ("What can happen?"). Rather than thinking of what could go wrong, they should think about what could go right. Participants are encouraged to set aside limiting beliefs and the unhelpful emotions associated with them, including pride, guilt, anxiety, and defensiveness.

It is completely normal for there to be skeptics in the group who either do not understand the exercise or are unsure of its value. As long as they agree to go through it in good faith, this should not cause a problem. The overwhelming majority of the time, the people will follow the example of their leaders. If everyone can tell that the leadership has authentically bought into the process, most doubters will come around quickly.

Traveling Forward

During this phase, I ask the group to enter an imaginary time machine and travel to a time in the near future that we have agreed upon, usually between three to five years ahead. It is often useful to use some theatrics in the set-up of future travel, like organizing a "future date" New Year's Eve Party to kick-off the exercise. There are other possibilities, so use your imagination for any sort of future event and have fun!

Once in the future setting, I ask them to begin to visualize what their company would look like in that time period if everything were perfect. I encourage them to identify specific criteria to describe and evaluate. These could include things like the products and services being offered by the company, sales, production, marketing, customer base, delivery, and so on.

Participants should then begin to imagine and describe what each of these criteria looks like in this future reality. With larger organizations, participants can be divided into smaller groups for this stage of the exercise. It is vital that the discussion take place "in" the future time, with participants fully imagining themselves present in the year being discussed. Descriptions should be as realistic and detailed as possible, which means that if someone describes a 10 percent increase in profits, for example, he or she must be able to describe definable sources for this increase that make sense to everyone in the group.

Of course bold visions of the future can be both exciting and scary. Tremendous success brings with it a host of new problems and responsibilities. Ideally, we look for visions that are equal parts scary and exciting: bold enough to be challenging, but still realistic for the time frame being discussed. Remember, the bolder the vision of the future, the more motivated people are to get there.

To maximize the effectiveness of the exercise, each person present should participate. Each individual comes from a different point of view and will have something different to contribute. By allowing

So this is what the future looks like!

themselves to explore a new place together, everyone will begin asking different questions and of course getting different answers.

Looking Back

Now the task is to look back on the past three to five years from the ideal future and ask the question "How did we get here?" Each person can answer that question based on his personal perspective of the company. What happened in the marketing department to get us to this ideal point? What did the product engineers do to get us here? What about accounting and sales?

Again, it is crucial that the dialogue continue to take place during the imagined future time period. We are very conditioned to plan from where we are to where we want to go, and this exercise deliberately disrupts that thinking process. It presupposes success, and allows us to look backward to map out the big steps it took to get us to our destination.

During this stage, most companies will determine the five most important action steps (although you can choose a different number) that brought the company from where they "were" to that "ideal" place in the future. There is a great deal of flexibility in how this can actually be done. I have led groups through sentence completion exercises, storytelling, artistic renderings, and even theatrical enactments to determine the steps.

Depending on company circumstances, you can choose to work by department or function, or likewise intermix roles for more diversity of ideas. Remember these are large steps, not day-to-day details. The facilitator in each group can keep everyone on task, and the leader of the overall exercise can circulate to ensure that no group gets mired down in the minutiae.

Planning from the future is not a magic trick or a gimmick. Done correctly, it simply offers any group the unique opportunity to alter their perspective and benefit from every member's insight, wisdom, and creativity. It stimulates bold and disruptive thinking in a way that few other activities are able to.

Back to Work

Now the leadership team has what it needs to begin constructing a more detailed tactical strategy. It is their task to move from the broad overview of the strategy to concrete steps that convert it into practical action. Normally, this tactical strategy will cover a 12- to 18-month period.

This is a fine-tuning process that will look very different depending on the various characteristics of the organization. In a small- or medium-sized company, it may only involve a handful of projects. In a larger or more complex organization, however, this process may involve several strategic initiatives, each encompassing multiple projects.

Whatever the scope of the actions planned at this stage, the leadership can go forward with the confidence that they have buy-in from the broader company, not just themselves. Rather than imposing a vision and strategy from the top, they will be implementing the collective vision of the entire group. Then the leaders truly become the servants of the group, as George Prince urged in his 1969 article mentioned in the last chapter.

It is also very important to determine how the progress toward these goals will be measured. This can be done with standard profit and loss assessments or key performance indicators. Many organizations may choose to utilize the Balanced Scorecard, developed by

Robert Kaplan and David Norton of Harvard Business School. This tool measures both financial and non-financial performance. This can be very helpful, because financial indicators can take several months to change after major changes have been made to an organization's vision or strategy.

Of course the plan will need to be adjusted and tweaked during the implementation process. Events that no one could have anticipated will inevitably occur, some of which may seem to disrupt the plan or throw it off course. But these need not be anything more than temporary detours on a path that has already been carefully charted.

The time machine exercise brings together many of the techniques and ideas for encouraging and cultivating creativity that we have discussed throughout this book, getting everyone to think in terms of limitless possibilities instead of limiting fears. If the exercise has been done properly, everyone will emerge with a clear vision that they can not only articulate, but can also see, feel, and own. Many companies find it useful to name the initiative or transformation, branding it internally to remind everyone what they saw and felt during the exercise itself.

Many authors and filmmakers will tell you that, during the creative process, they begin their stories with the ending and work backward to make sure the plot takes them where they want to go. This is because any complicated story has to be started with the end in mind; otherwise, the narrative may take unexpected turns that lead to an unsatisfying resolution.

The time machine technique works the same way, telling the story of your company's next few years with the end in mind. And anyone who has tried it will tell you that it works remarkably well. In fact, a growing body of evidence suggests that much of the way we make sense of the world is through stories. In the next chapter, we'll look more closely at the stories we tell about ourselves, and how we can change them to get the ending we want.

Nine

Creating Coincidences

ON JULY 4, 1826, John Adams, the second president of the United States, and Thomas Jefferson, the third president, died exactly 50 years after both men had signed the Declaration of Independence. Biographer B.L. Rayner wrote of the event, "The extraordinary coincidence in the death of these great men is without parallel in the records of history."[1]

The most straightforward definition of "coincidence" is two or more events occurring simultaneously. Of course it has also come to mean two things happening at the same time in a way that is both remarkable and apparently unplanned by the people involved. For example, you find out you are going to have a baby, and you see a maternity shop down the street from your office. Is this a random occurrence, or is it part of some larger plan?

Psychiatrist Carl Jung coined the term "synchronicity" to describe meaningful coincidences. Jung viewed such phenomena as communication from a transcendent realm, although many skeptics disagree. The view of Jung's critics is summarized succinctly by Benjamin Radford, author of *Scientific Paranormal Investigation: How to Solve Unexplained Mysteries:* "The appearance of synchronicity is the result of a well-known psychological phenomenon called confirmation bias . . . we much more easily notice and remember things that confirm our beliefs than those that do not. The human brain is very good at making connections and seeing designs in ambiguous stimuli and random patterns."[2]

As Radford explains, confirmation bias is our tendency to pay attention to information that confirms what we already believe and ignore information that contradicts it. It's the reason we tend to think the penalties called on our favorite sports team are unjustified, but the penalties called on our opponents are completely reasonable. It is also the reason a coffee lover will eagerly read an article about how coffee might help delay the onset of Alzheimer's disease but ignore one about how it can be associated with headaches. This very human tendency affects everyone regardless of age, race, education level or political persuasion. A study by Ohio State University released in February 2015, for example, revealed that both liberals and conservatives were biased against scientific findings that did not align with their political views.[3]

The idea that even remarkable coincidences could be chalked up to confirmation bias is not as farfetched as it might seem. For example, if you are looking for a job in Houston, we don't think of it as a remarkable coincidence if you find a job in Houston. You looked for something, and you found it. In the same way, you only noticed the maternity shop after you found out you were having a baby. Chances are, that store was always right there, you just never paid any attention. Once you found out you were expecting, you may not have been intentionally looking for the store, but your subconscious mind was.

Confirmation bias understandably receives a bad rap: it can lead us to all sorts of irrational beliefs and prejudices. However, the tendency of our brains to look for patterns and our interpretations of coincidences that come with it are not all bad news. Our brains need to make sense of the world to conserve our time and mental energy. If we had to sit down and think carefully and dispassionately through an exhaustive pros and cons list before every decision in our day, we would never get anything done. Additionally, we can also have a tendency to notice and pay attention to the things in the world that are associated to achieving the

You know, ever since you've been pregnant there seem to be maternity shops on every corner!

goals and desired results we are actively visualizing. We will explore more on that later in the chapter.

Building Mental Models

So how does our brain decide what to notice and what to ignore? The reticular activating system (RAS) is sometimes described as the gateway through which most sensory information enters the brain. Although much of the RAS is associated with sleep to wake transitions, it also regulates our attention. Extending from the brainstem to the midbrain, the RAS calls certain stimuli to our attention, while allowing us to overlook others.

Perhaps one of the most powerful illustrations of the RAS in action is a mother's ability to hear her child's voice in the midst of a crowded, noisy room. It's also the part of the brain that allowed you to ignore the maternity shops until you found out you were having a baby. But how does our RAS decide what is worthy of our attention?

The answer goes back to Dr. Kahneman's "two systems" that we discussed earlier. System 1 is the subconscious: effortless, quick, and intuitive. System 2 is the conscious part of our brain: deliberate, effortful, and slow. For better or for worse, the overwhelming majority of our subconscious mind is programmed from birth to about six years old.[4] It is during this time period, through observing the people in our lives and the world around us, that it develops mental models of how the world works. These include, but are not limited to, identities, stereotypes, and worldviews, and not all of these models are equally helpful or accurate.[5]

Although all mental models are generalizations, some lead to better outcomes than others. For example, let's say Carl and Marco have identical abilities. Carl's parents, however, did not go to college nor do they care if he does. Carl's subconscious has thus developed a mental model that tells him that higher education is not very important. Marco's parents, on the other hand, both went to college and his mother has a master's degree. Marco subconsciously believes that higher education is very valuable. Without really thinking about why, Marco will probably work much harder in high school than Carl will.

In order to "reprogram" Carl's unhelpful subconscious mental model, it is necessary for Carl's System 2 to override his System 1. To do this, he must identify the unhelpful belief and begin to deliberately replace it with a different one. Any of the meditation methods, visualization techniques, and the Time Machine exercises we discussed in the last chapter can be very helpful in this process. But how do these subconsciously held beliefs influence our creativity?

The Subconscious and Creativity

However much we may need to enlist System 2 to critically examine System 1's cherished beliefs and assumptions now and then, both System 1 and 2 play important roles in the creative process. As Scott Barry Kaufman explains in *Scientific American*, "The entire creative process—from preparation to incubation to illumination to verification—consists of many interacting cognitive processes (both conscious and unconscious) and emotions. Depending on the stage of the creative process, and *what* you're actually attempting to create, different brain regions are recruited to handle the task."[6]

Kaufman is referring to researcher Graham Wallis's model of the creative process, which involved four stages:

1. *Preparation:* where the need or problem is clearly defined and researched.
2. *Incubation:* where the problem is contemplated.
3. *Illumination:* where ideas—whole or partial—arise in the mind and are contemplated in response to the need or problem.
4. *Verification:* where activities and experiments are conducted to verify that a solution has indeed been obtained.

In our success spiral model from Chapter 4, the preparation, incubation, and illumination stages would correspond roughly to Beliefs, Potential, and First Creation and the verification to Second Creation. Kaufman also explains that, according to the Dual-Process theory of Human Intelligence, System 1 and System 2 are equally important to both intelligence and creativity. The important thing, according to Kaufman, is to be able to switch between the two depending on what the task demands.[7]

Many great authors find their subconscious playing a much greater role in their writing than they initially realize. J.R.R. Tolkien, the father of modern fantasy and creator of the vast and multilayered world of Middle Earth, was a devout Catholic. He did not, however, set out to write fantasy novels imbued with

Catholic imagery and symbolism. When questioned about this, Tolkien explained, *"The Lord of the Rings* is of course a fundamentally religious and Catholic work; unconsciously so at first, but consciously in the revision. . . . For as a matter of fact, I have consciously planned very little; and should chiefly be grateful for having been brought up (since I was eight) in a Faith that has nourished me and taught me all the little that I know; and that I owe to my mother . . ."[8]

Author John Boyne, who rarely plans his novels, explained, "I think a lot of my writing comes from the subconscious . . . when I write I start with an idea for a scene or a character and just see where it takes me."[9] But not planning is not a prerequisite for the influence of the subconscious on the creative process. Author Michelle Paver is known for meticulously planning her novels, yet she agrees with Boyne, "Even if you plan your book, the actual writing is unplanned. All stories come from the subconscious—which is why it doesn't make sense to over-plan."[10]

Nor is the subconscious influence solely found among authors. Arthur Fry, one of the inventors of the Post-it note, explained, "I back away from conscious thought and turn the problem over to my unconscious mind. It will scan a broader array of patterns and find some new close fits from other information stored in my brain." Again, that subconscious includes all our thoughts and experiences, but also the mental models we have built to understand the world.

Identity: The Ultimate Mental Model

Identity can be thought of as the subconscious mental model we develop of ourselves. From the time we become self-aware (a gradual transition most psychologists believe happens between ages one and three[11]), we struggle to discover and define who and what we are. Are we merely highly advanced animals, or do we possess a soul that will go on living after our bodies have disintegrated? Were we created or are we somehow self-existent? What does our human existence mean, and what is its purpose?

How we answer these questions often takes on the form of a story. Psychologist Dan P. McAdams explains that only in the 1980s did psychologists begin to understand the value that our self-constructed "life stories" have for understanding human behavior. He further argues that our very identities take on the form of a story, complete with a setting, characters, a plot, and themes.

McAdams explains, "In late adolescence and young adulthood, people living in modern societies begin to reconstruct the personal past, perceive the present, and anticipate the future in terms of an internalized and evolving self-story, an integrated narrative of self that provides modern life with some modicum of psychosocial unity and purpose."[12]

According to McAdams, while these "self-stories" are based on facts, they go far beyond real events. We remember some things and forget others. We sub-consciously decide what role we play in the story: the hero, the villain, the victim, the martyr. We decide what roles the other characters play as well.

These roles, themes, and settings are not static; they can change over time, and often do. For example, most of us remember a transitional period from adolescence—when we likely saw our parents in the role of antagonists—to adulthood, when many of them became our heroes. But the longer we live, the more we begin to bend and squeeze the realities of our lives to fit into the narrative we have already created, not because it necessarily makes us happy, but because it makes sense.[13] We find comfort in repeating a familiar story, even if that story is not a particularly happy one.

Discovering and deliberately aligning with one's true identity can be a transformational experience in fulfilling one's creative, personal, and professional potential. Nearly two decades ago I worked with a client, "Patricia," who was the managing director for the Scandinavian operations of a global pharmaceutical company. She was a classic "wunderkind," rising from an entry-level marketing job to this new position in record time. She was brimming with confidence and fresh ideas, yet she felt strangely dissatisfied with her work. After speaking with her, I knew just the exercise she needed to address her dissatisfaction.

Neurological Level Alignment is a very specific exercise based on the Neuro-Linguistic Programming discussed in the last chapter. It is a pragmatic approach to making sense of all these nagging questions that are identified by psychologists, theologians, and philosophers, but not always satisfactorily addressed. Ultimately, the exercise cleanly links one's current or desired behavior with a deeper sense of identity and meaning.

The NLA exercise is based on the assumption that people are able to align their actions with their abilities, with their beliefs and values, and with their sense of identity and purpose. When any of these components are out of alignment, we can feel unfulfilled, unfocused, stressed out, or even angry. When we are in these less-than-optimum mental or emotional states, our performance is not at its peak, which in turn affects our results. Most of us intuitively understand this. We know we feel frustrated if our jobs involve tasks that are far too easy or far too difficult. We feel guilty or uncomfortable if we are asked to do something that does not align with our values or beliefs.

But what happens when we are out of alignment with our sense of identity and purpose? When we have not taken the time to examine in great depth the stories we tell ourselves, we may find ourselves constantly doing things that disrupt our innermost being without realizing it. This often leads to frustration or dissatisfaction with a job that seems to match us perfectly on paper.

Through a series of movements and questions, coachees are guided to discover which areas of their lives are out of alignment and what to do about it. I took Patricia through these steps, and when we got to the questions about identity, she responded with conviction: "I am a pastor!" In every area of her life—her work, her family, and her community involvement—she shepherded and protected people. She made sure they were safe and had what they needed to thrive and grow.

This was a transformational moment for Patricia. Suddenly, all the different roles she played in all different facets of her life made sense. This understanding clarified her goals and helped her to prioritize how she allocated her time and energy. Not long after our session, she became the youngest general director and won a prestigious leadership award from the company. And after a time of success at that position, as well as growing to serve at some of the highest global positions in the company, she ultimately went on to become the CEO of a well-known international cosmetics company.

Today, Patricia is known for being a high-energy leader who is deeply connected to her higher purpose, and she is just one of many great corporate leaders who trace their success to discovering and aligning with their true identity. I have consistently found that those I coach, including many Fortune 500 CEOs, come out of NLA sessions more confident, with a clearer sense of what they believe, and identifying with their higher purpose. They find it cleansing and powerful, and some call it the most powerful and meaningful exercise they have ever participated in.

This secure sense of identity will also set us up for many more positive coincidences. When we understand our abilities and our role in a larger "story," we are much more likely to find the right opportunities to fulfill that role. A self-aware "pastor" like Patricia is more likely to "coincidentally" bump into the sheep that need shepherding than someone who might possess the same gifts but be unaware of them. Likewise, a "trailblazer" who knows he is meant to go where others have not gone before will probably "coincidentally" find the supplies and comrades he needs for his journey.

The Expectations Game

After you have aligned your various neurological levels with your identity and sense of purpose, the next step in preparing your subconscious mind for the right coincidences is managing your expectations. Imagine two servers preparing to work the same shift in the same restaurant. The first wakes up and thinks, "I hate this restaurant. The customers are so cheap; they never tip well." The second wakes up and thinks, "I know my customers are not wealthy, but I know they will be generous to me." At the end of the shift, the first server has indeed received an average of 10 percent on his sales, while the second server has received closer to 16 percent on hers.

Both servers might view their outcomes as coincidences. Negative people in particular often have trouble seeing the connection between their expectations and their outcomes. But it isn't too difficult to see how the first server's expectations will color his attitude, subconsciously causing him to treat customers with less care and in turn causing them to give smaller tips. The second server's decision to expect the best from her customers will cause her to give better service, and on average receive better tips.

Of course the first server could get some generous customers who tip well regardless of the service, and the second could get some stingy customers who do the opposite. But over the course of time the second server will certainly receive more money than the first. So it is with expectations in general; expecting positive outcomes won't cause every interaction to go perfectly every time. But over the long haul you will find much better results than if you are constantly expecting the worst.

Now high expectations are not necessarily a magical path to a happy life. In fact, unrealistically high expectations often lead to disappointment. If the second server had expected a 50-dollar tip on every 20-dollar check, she was bound to feel disheartened after a while. Unrealistically high expectations can also have a negative effect on creativity. In his book *The Accidental Creative: How to be Brilliant at a Moment's Notice,* author Todd Henry explains how allowing one's expectations to be shaped by comparison with the performance or abilities of others—even extremely inspiring individuals—can unintentionally inhibit creativity.

Henry explains, "The moment we place concrete expectations on the end results of a project—this upgrade is going to double last year's sales figures!—we begin closing off potential executions and helpful thoughts because we deem them 'not useful enough' in accomplishing our escalated expectations. Doing this too early in the creative process can seriously derail brilliant ideas and prevent them from ever seeing the light of day."[14]

He goes on to describe three main sources of this kind of negative effect: our past work, our managers and colleagues, and our innovation heroes. The problem with comparing ideas as they come to us with those of others or even with our own completed projects is that ideas often emerge initially in an undeveloped or partial form. We may dismiss them because they are not fully formed, instead of working to develop them into something more complete.

So to be healthy and successful, individuals must actively construct both a compelling and realistic vision of the future so as to balance expectations, and then pay close attention to the empowering coincidences they pursue. Please keep in mind: expectations do have to be tempered by the time frame we are exploring. Generally speaking, we tend to overestimate what we are capable of achieving in the short term, and thus risk suffering disappointment due to unrealistic expectations. And likewise, we tend to greatly underestimate what we are capable of achieving in the long term, and thus sell ourselves short of our true potential. So think BIG about your longer-term aspirations and maintain a realistic mindset about the steps to get you there. Here are some practical guidelines to move forward in a balanced and constructive manner.

1. *Use visualization techniques to set yourself up for meaningful coincidences.* In his book *As a Man Thinketh*, James Allen said, "There is an unavoidable tendency to become literally the embodiment of that quality upon which one most constantly thinks."[15] Our minds notice and pay attention to the stimuli around us that are in some way associated with what we are thinking about, and the practice of visualization focuses the mind at a very deep level. On the physiological level, the same neural networks fire when you are being pricked with a pin, watching someone be pricked with a pin, or remembering the experience of being pricked with a pin (although they will fire with less intensity in the latter two cases).

What this means is that there is a part of us that actually believes that our visualization is true. Consequently, we tend to start seeing, hearing, and feeling just what we need to move closer to our visualized state. Like suddenly seeing the maternity shops in our example of discovering you are going to be a parent, we unconsciously search for what we need to support what we think about and expect. Peter McWilliams put it very nicely when he said, "To visualize is to see what is not there, what is not real— a dream. To visualize is, in fact, to make visual lies. Visual lies, however, have a way of coming true."[16]

2. *Remember to keep your visualizations rooted in reality by acting diligently to achieve them.* People are often told that if they visualize the things they want, this will enable their brains to "attract" those things, and filter out everything else. Some will go so far as to say that if you want to drive a red sports car, you should visualize a red sports car on a regular and systematic basis. Now it is true that you will then probably begin to notice more red sports cars on the road, so in that sense you are "creating coincidences." But ultimately, limiting yourself to only fantasizing about owning a red sports

car will not bring you any closer to being able to purchase one if you don't have the money. You need to keep yourself attentive to other collateral coincidences you might find around you that will help you develop a tactical strategy to obtain the means to buy it, and then act on those tactics. That may even mean that a seemingly unrelated coincidence brings along a helpful opportunity that takes you another step closer to actually purchasing the car.

3. *Create a vision board.* Priming the subconscious for creative revelation and professional success is about filling your mind with ideas. You want to saturate your mind with carefully selected words and images that do more than just conjure up a good feeling; they should feed the actual process of creation. Some people do this by creating bulletin boards or books (physical or electronic) filled with words and images associated with what they are trying to accomplish. This can help your subconscious mind recognize important information and opportunities and draw them to your attention.

4. *Check your motivations.* Psychologist Theresa Amabile expounds on the importance of being motivated by forces like love and curiosity rather than money or fame: "When

people are intrinsically motivated, they engage in their work for the challenge and enjoyment of it. The work *itself* is motivating . . . people will be most creative when they feel motivated primarily by the interest, satisfaction, and challenge of the work itself—and not by external pressures."[17] When you have been through an NLA exercise, or something similar, you can sense an increase in your motivation toward the work itself, because it will be aligned with what you believe and who you are.

During the process of writing this book, I was scheduled to be in Clearwater with the CFO of an international tech firm. Clearwater is just a short flight from my home in West Palm Beach. On countless occasions, I have left at 7 a.m. for meetings there and been at home eating my dinner by 7 p.m.

That particular morning when I took my seat on the small propeller plane, rain was coming down by the bucketful. After several minutes, the pilot announced that we would be delayed until some extreme weather moved out of our flight path. Minutes turned into hours, however, and by the time the plane actually left the runway, I had had to cancel my meeting and return home.

When I rescheduled the meeting with the CFO, I learned that the new date happened to coincide with a trip that a colleague of mine, "Bill," was making to Clearwater as well. I had introduced him to my contacts at the same tech firm, and he was scheduled to meet with them that day. As we made plans to meet up while we were there, Bill mentioned that he had another meeting in the Clearwater area first thing that morning. This meeting was with a senior leader of one of the largest HR services firms in the world, and he invited me to come along.

What I might have viewed as an extremely annoying inconvenience—being rained out of my original meeting—became an open door for an incredible business opportunity. In a way, this was a remarkable coincidence, and certainly a positive one. But in another way, it was a natural outworking of the mutually beneficial relationship that I have with Bill and that I have been blessed to have with many others. We create our own coincidences by building relationships, thinking boldly, believing that all is possible, visualizing, and by being very attentive to what is actually happening right in front of us.

In the next chapter, we'll explore how the Bold Mind model allows for a radical rethinking of professional relationships between individuals, departments, and even companies.

Ten

Transforming Relationships

"IN SHORT, THE NEW model promises to increase both our market share and our profit margins in an extremely competitive time," the senior leader of the electronics manufacturing company (Omicron) explained to me. We were debriefing from the transformation of their relationship with one of their distributors (Syne Technologies) that had been 12 months in the making. To bring the two companies to that point, I had been working together with various members of their respective leadership teams to embrace a new kind of collaborative relationship. Obviously, I was incredibly relieved that the results of the activity in their respective businesses were meeting their expectations.

But nothing could have prepared me for what he said next: "You know what, Scott?" he added, "Even if that time we spent together wasn't producing any tangible business results—even if it wasn't promising to increase our margins at all—I would still have done it anyway. It has made coming to work so much more pleasant. Our companies are enjoying so much synergy right now, and that alone has been worth it. In fact, I can't quite explain it, but somehow the energy of what we did in that exercise has run over to improve the relationships we enjoy with other distributors as well!"

Of course part of me wanted to laugh at this remarkable statement. These kinds of leaders were typically driven by numbers (quarterly earnings, stock prices, and so on). They were obsessed with keeping costs low and income high. Yet this man had found that a shift in mindset had not only brought him a potentially better business, but also transformed the way he and his company related to others.

A New Era

Ironically, before the series of meetings I directed between Omicron and Syne Technologies, the two firms were facing yet another in a series of seemingly endless crises in their decades-old partnership. The profit margins for both companies were incredibly tight, and they were largely controlled by the leaders of Omicron who determined what Syne would ultimately pay for the products, while the market determined what they could charge their customers. Syne wasn't the only distributor Omicron worked with, but they were by far the largest and most important for their segment in the regional market.

The leaders of Syne made it clear to me that they had felt unfairly challenged and pressured in previous agreements. The annual renegotiations were always heated, but they were further complicated by the complexity of the models Omicron used to determine what Syne would actually be able to earn. Both Syne and Omicron were under immense pressure to show quarterly profits to their boards and shareholders, and by the time we all sat down together both groups were incredibly frustrated. Although both companies needed each other to survive, neither seemed willing to budge.

Increased specialization—of individuals and of companies—is the mark of a dynamic and complex society. A hundred years ago, nearly everyone went to a family doctor to treat almost any kind of ailment. Today you have specialists for every body system and almost every medical procedure. The same is true with companies. Rather than a corporate landscape filled with self-sufficient giants, we have multitudes of companies, many of which may carry out just one small part of a production or delivery process.

This trend toward increased specialization has led to much greater efficiency, and doubtless consumers benefit immensely from lower prices and an ever increasing variety of products and services to choose from. Along the way, however, collaboration—both for sustainable business practices and for innovation—has become more than a nice idea. It has become an absolute necessity for survival.

But that does not mean it is easy, particularly when two or more individuals or companies must collaborate on multiple levels to achieve the needed outcome. Writing in *Harvard Business Review*, Heidi Gardner explains some of the challenges of multidisciplinary collaboration: "It's different from mere assembly . . . and from sequential, interdependent projects. . . . True multidisciplinary collaboration requires people to combine their perspectives and expertise and tailor them to the client's (or the market's) needs so that the outcome is more than the sum of the participating individuals' knowledge."[1]

Yet despite these challenges, the future clearly holds more such collaboration on every level, not less. Consider that immensely innovative and successful undertakings like Wikipedia—the completely free online encyclopedia that anyone can edit—were developed by harnessing what many refer to as "collaborative intelligence." Rather than dozens or hundreds of full-time employees, Wikipedia relies on millions of passionate volunteers. Although they may not have the academic credibility of a publication like the *Encyclopedia Britannica*, they are arguably more relevant and their content is undeniably exploding. As of this writing, the English portion of Wikipedia expands at the rate of 10 edits per second and about 800 new articles a day. It is the sixth most popular website in the world, recording more than 186 million daily hits.[2]

In this kind of collaborative effort no one owns the content, and the people who do the work do it for nonmonetary rewards. They donate their time because they enjoy writing about interesting topics or because they are passionate about a particular subject. Google was one of the first examples of a for-profit company that has been able to harness the power of this kind of collaboration, allowing page hits rather than paid marketing experts to determine which content is relevant to whom. Any forward-thinking entrepreneur can see that this kind of collaboration will only become more prevalent in the future.

Meaningful collaboration is ultimately impossible for people who view creative energy as a finite commodity. If you believe that the creativity and ideas of others somehow take away from the uniqueness or importance of your own, then you will never be able to combine efforts effectively with anyone else. If you believe your own well of creative resources is exhaustible, you will approach interactions and opportunities by trying to secure what you are being given before you offer anything of value to anyone else. This mindset has led to many dysfunctional relationships, both between individuals and between companies.

The Default Business Relationship

Businesses can have any number of different types of cooperative relationships with one another. They can be strategic partners, vendor-client, supplier-retailer, or manufacturer-distributor, just to name a few. Unfortunately, for various reasons many companies in these kind of relationships still behave like competitors.

This problem comes from the tendency of most leaders to view any kind of business transaction as a zero-sum game. If I give you more out of the deal, then I am getting less. In the simplest possible terms, it may be true that giving your partner more now means less for you in the immediate future. If I offer you a larger margin on an item I produce and you distribute, that leaves less money on the table for me. This reality leads the parties involved to try to squeeze as much as they can out of each other while giving up as little as possible. This might make sense to shareholders, but it rarely makes for a productive long-term relationship.

The zero-sum game mindset leads to many unhelpful behaviors that have little to do with money. Companies may battle for control of certain processes for the sake of control itself. They may argue over relatively unimportant things, like whose logo appears at the top of the page on the letterhead or which company name appears first in a press release. And of course they may argue over any number of details in the formalized agreement between the parties. Through time this can lead to unnecessary aggravation, wasted time, and even the dissolution of the relationship.

Sometimes the needs of the two companies change enough that the partnership no longer makes economic sense. But most collaborative breakups boil down to the relationships between individuals that ultimately undergird the relationship between the companies. Disagreements or even apparently conflicting interests are not problems in and of themselves; these can almost always be resolved respectfully. But a breakdown in the personal relationships—particularly between the leaders—can be deadly to an otherwise productive partnership.

Writing in *Forbes*, Amanda Neville cites five major signs that a business partnership is doomed: 1) when leaders cannot reach a detailed partnership agreement; 2) when the tasks or duties are grossly uneven: 3) when the financial values of the companies are too different; 4) when the leaders are unable to disagree in a productive way; and 5) when the two companies cannot agree on standard operating policy. Neville explains, "If you can't come to a consensus about policies, you're in trouble. And if you have a consensus but one or more people feels disrespected or undermined, you're still in trouble because you compromised too much."[3]

Partnerships in business have much in common with a marriage or other relationships between two individuals. Although there are multitudes of reasons given for divorce, almost all can be traced to the breakdown of communication and a lack of trust. Restore communication and trust, and you will restore the health of the relationship.

The Bold Mind Model

I knew exactly what Omicron and Syne needed to do to end the continued standoff and find a way of working together that would make everyone happy. Yet I was afraid that neither company was going to go for it. As with almost any kind of relationship counseling, whether it is personal or professional, the problem at hand is not that either party lacks information. Spouses know they are supposed to respect each other and share common interests, but that doesn't mean they know how to do it. In the same way, everyone knows that you are supposed to try to negotiate a "win-win" outcome, but very few are able to get it done.

On a business level, the problems between Omicron and Syne were very complicated; their industry was changing rapidly and their profit margins were razor thin. But that wasn't why they were having so much trouble reaching a mutually agreeable working dynamic. The stress from their very real business issues had caused a breakdown in trust and communication between the leaders of both companies. And like everyone who fights over the size of their piece of the pie, what they really needed to do was figure out how to bake a bigger pie. But they would have to do this together, and for that they needed to create a bold vision of a shared future while rebuilding trust and communication.

After some very diligent planning and negotiating, we were able to gather together the leadership teams from each company in a conference room on neutral ground near a major airport. There I began to implement the Bold Mind model for transforming business relationships. This model is based on a completely different set of assumptions from those of the default business relationship. First, it assumes that every organization has an unlimited supply of creative energy and unlimited potential for innovation. Second, it supposes that this energy multiplies when two or more organizations connect in a trusting relationship. Thus, such organizations can work together in a way that leaves both of them much better off than they would be otherwise. The key is to develop a shared vision of a compelling future together.

First, I addressed the challenges both companies had faced in the past. Their nearly two decades of a theoretically cooperative but competitive relationship had left both sides with emotional baggage that included everything from annoyance and bruised egos to feelings of distrust. I acknowledged all these issues and challenged both sides to set them aside for the sake of what we were trying to accomplish.

Second, I acknowledged that exposing what each company really needed required a degree of vulnerability. When we share what we really want, we give others the tools to hurt us. I knew this would be a tall order for all the individuals present, but I challenged them to try.

Third, I cast a new vision for what their partnership could be. Hybrid cars, I explained, typically have two engines: a classic internal combustion engine, which runs on gasoline, and an electric engine, which runs on a battery. I explained how the two engines complement each other; the electrical motor draws on the battery to pull away from a stop, while the internal combustion engine takes over at cruising speed when it is most efficient. During this time, the internal combustion engine also powers a generator that charges the battery of the electrical engine. A special transmission allows both engines to work together to accelerate the car with their combined power when necessary. The result is a car that takes its driver where he wants to go with unparalleled efficiency.

I explained to everyone in the room that up to this point, the relationship between their two companies had been like two engines in a hybrid car that were occasionally fighting against one another, pulling in different directions. The goal, I explained, was to become a hybrid team that supported one another and consistently pulled in the same direction. If they could learn to function this way, I promised that both companies would get where they wanted to go much more efficiently.

A Fresh Start

To my infinite relief, both leadership teams embraced this new concept, at least enough to try it. It was almost as if they had been waiting for someone to suggest such a course of action—a way forward that promised a better business for both. I then took them through a modified version of the Time Machine Experience discussed in Chapter 8. Now that each party understood clearly where the other was and what the other

We can really build something great together working as a Hybrid Team!

needed, they were ready to begin designing their ideal future together. This included where they wanted their sales, product development, margins, and market share.

We also went through the process of developing a team charter, which specified the purpose of the team, the role of each member, the values, and guiding principles. Together, we outlined the objectives and specific KPIs we would be monitoring. All this was done with buy-in from everyone in the room.

The vision that this new hybrid team produced was a plan to double their volume of business (which was in the billions already) while also doubling their profit margins. This was a bold vision and a risky plan heading into an unknown future, but they laid out the details for where the added volume would come from in their various areas of business.

We then split the nearly 20 individuals present into four subgroups with members from both companies. Each team took the time to clearly define what the ideal future looked like for their respective business units, and for their relationship as a whole. As I looked around the room, I recognized that the willingness to move forward with this kind of process took great courage on the part of both leadership teams. They had to embrace a radically different view of their relationship moving forward, which required risk—both professional and emotional—on both sides.

Just like in the Time Machine Experience, each group then began planning the big steps that they needed to take in the next two years to get to the ideal future they had previously described. As part of the new plan, both companies agreed to relax some of the stringent quarterly targets that had been causing the tremendous stress over short-term outcomes, and jointly focus on shared success.

By the end of the day, something truly remarkable had happened. Not only were the interactions warmer, more comfortable, and even punctuated by laughter, but all the people in the room were speaking in terms of "we." And that "we" meant both companies in the partnership. They had truly become a hybrid team, fueling one another and pulling together in the same direction.

Keys to Transforming Relationships

I have since repeated this kind of process with many different companies in a variety of cooperative relationships. Although no two companies are alike, and thus no two relationships between companies are alike, there are some general steps that will help improve the way your company relates to potential partners, vendors, suppliers, distributors, clients, and so on.

Assess Your Organization

To collaborate well with others, you need to have a realistic assessment of your company's strengths and weaknesses, as well as of your capabilities and disabilities. Evaluating these areas should include assessing your resources, such as the people you employ, your equipment, your relationships, your brand strength, and your customer base. It should also include determining the strength of your production, communication, and decision-making processes.

Without this information, you will not be able to plan realistically and effectively, nor will you be able to identify which kinds of organizations would make good collaborative partners. It can sometimes be helpful to employ an external professional to help you with this evaluation process.

Assess Your Potential Partner

You will want to know not only the capabilities and disabilities of your potential partner organization, but you will also want to understand their values, guiding principles, and mission. These do not have to be identical to those of your company, but they do need to be compatible.

Articulate Expectations

As we discussed in the last chapter, our sense of well-being is not determined solely by how well things go. It is determined by how well things go compared to how well we expected them to go. This is why it is important at the beginning of any partnership for each party to articulate its expectations in as much detail as possible. This allows both partners to offer corrections or modifications to expectations at the beginning and thus avoid unnecessary disappointment or misunderstandings later.

If you have an existing partnership and have never gone through this process, you may want to simply call a meeting to get it done. Unarticulated expectations can kill collaborative relationships just as they can kill personal ones. The sooner you get them out on the table, the better.

Create an Integrated Work Environment

Collaboration should not feel like an extra burden for your employees. Whenever possible, create a platform that allows your employees to work with the partner with ease and harmony. Communication should flow effortlessly, and it should become second nature to build something great together.

Create a Collaborative Partner Organization

Sometimes it actually makes sense to create or "spin off" a separate organization with which your company can then collaborate. This can be particularly true if you have an established customer base but also want to develop new products or services for markets that may not yet exist. In his book *The Innovator's Dilemma*, author Clayton Christensen makes the case that an established organization will struggle if it tries to serve a mainstream customer base while simultaneously trying to develop disruptive technologies. He theorizes that it is customers who allocate a company's resources much more than its management, and advocates creating a separate organization whose customers need disruptive technology. This allows the "new" organization to be market-driven and disruptive at the same time.

Consider Rotating Leadership of Projects

Many partnerships benefit from rotating control of projects rather than sharing it. This prevents one company leading the entire time and becoming overly dominant, but it also avoids the inefficiencies that can come with shared leadership.

Monitor the Metrics That Matter

Make sure that both partners agree on metrics from the beginning, so that success is clearly defined. Of course you will want to monitor all the typical KPIs, but you will also want to find ways to measure progress toward the specific benchmarks that you have set for your hybrid teams. Find ways to monitor long-term as well as short-term goals.

Acknowledge Disappointments and Frustrations Early

Nothing poisons a relationship like ignoring a problem and hoping it will go away on its own. When you set bold targets, you don't always reach them. If that happens after a quarter or two, acknowledge it and give everyone the opportunity to share their thoughts and feelings about it. This diffuses any tension before it has time to build up into a problem, and ensures that everyone stays on the same page.

Whenever Possible, Have Diverse Teams

Having team members from both companies is important, but having team members with a variety of perspectives is important too. For example, forming teams that have both men and women and introverts and extroverts can produce better results. A 2012 Credit Suisse study found that companies with at least one woman on their board perform better than those with all-male boards.[4]

Follow Up Regularly

One of the questions I am asked most frequently is how do I prevent the parties from falling back into their old ways after they have made so much progress? No matter how powerful the meeting was, there is always the danger of it becoming a pleasant but distant memory.

The answer is simple: Follow up diligently and often. In the case of Omicron and Syne, we brought the leadership teams of both companies back together for a face-to-face executive summit every six months. It is almost inevitable that the needs of any company will change over time. Regular meetings ensure that these changes do not catch anyone by surprise, and that agreements or logistics can be adjusted accordingly.

Done correctly, this kind of collaborative relationship will reduce stress in the workplace and increase the dopamine and serotonin that we all need in order to optimize our personal and collective creativity. Ultimately, our ability to cultivate the creativity that drives innovation is deeply affected by our worldview. Do we see ourselves clawing for a slightly larger piece of a pie of a fixed size, or do we see the world as full of endless possibilities? If we see the world from the first point of view, we will try to exploit potential partners as much as possible, while giving them as little in return as possible. If we see the world the second way, we will be open, vulnerable, and make the effort to come up with agreements and solutions that have the potential to provide both partners with the best possible outcomes.

Eleven

Unthinkable
New Ways

How do you create the future?

To begin to answer a virtually unanswerable question, it might help to take a quick look at a company that—decades ago—was busy creating the time period we are living in right now. Before Apple, Google, and countless other tech companies brought us incredible innovation, there was Bell Labs. Tucked away for decades on a surprisingly beautiful campus in suburban New Jersey, the company employed 15,000 scientists at its peak. Not exactly the tiny, nimble startup we're used to seeing today. Yet they produced more than 30,000 patents, many of which radically changed the world, and their scientists were awarded eight Nobel Prizes.

When it opened in 1925, Bell Labs (now owned by Nokia) was essentially the research and engineering arm of AT&T, America's telephone company. In the quest to connect the entire United States by telephone, they developed what felt like an endless variety of innovations including the laser, programming languages like C, the UNIX operating system, and the transistor. C and its extension C++ became two of the most widely used programming languages of all time. The first transistor, tested in December 1947, "was a quarter of the size of an American penny; now a computer-processor chip the size of a postage stamp contains 2 billion transistors. Intel makes 10 billion transistors every second. Who could have imagined it?"[1]

By 1960, the phone system stretched across the continent, and customers could dial long distance directly instead of depending on an operator. Rather than sit back and enjoy their virtual monopoly on telephone service, the leaders at Bell Labs focused on the growing needs of the network they had built. They anticipated three major demands in the near future: greater speed of communication, the ability to digitize more information, and the capacity to handle an increased volume of information traffic.[2] In their quest to meet those demands, they laid the groundwork for the completely interconnected world we live in today.

Innovation at Bell Labs was a three-stage process, explains Jon Gertner in his fascinating book *The Idea Factory: Bell Labs and the Great Age of American Innovation*. Scientists followed a pattern of "apprehending a vexing problem, gathering ideas that might lead to a solution, and then pushing toward the development of a product that could be deployed on a massive scale."[3] As they did this, they arguably released an unprecedented level of creative power, which continues to benefit us all to this day.

There are many "vexing problems" facing us in the decades ahead, from the need for sustainable energy in the face of a growing global population to the demand for security in light of various political and military threats. To dissect all of these complex issues lies far beyond the scope of this book. However, there are five major challenges on the horizon that will certainly play a significant role in shaping the future years and decades. The companies that will create the future understand these problems and which ones they are best suited to solve.

1. Connectivity

Since ancient times, human progress has been inexorably tied to the exchange of ideas. This is why more densely populated areas tended to advance and innovate more quickly. The more crowded areas around the Nile in Egypt, the Tigris and the Euphrates in

Mesopotamia, the Indus in India, and the Yellow River in China were the first places to develop writing, mathematics, and early forms of scientific inquiry. There were simply more human brains to put to work.

As time progressed, ideas were shared around the world through letters, telegraph, telephone calls, and finally email, internet forums, and instant messaging. These tremendous advances in technology have not only changed the way we can communicate, they have also changed the way we do business. Some companies have abandoned centralized offices all together, relying on virtual assistants, file-sharing platforms, and video conference calls.

In the current information age, the need to be able to connect instantly to another person, or group of people, is unlikely to change any time soon. The more cell phone users and the greater quantities of digital information that we need to send to one another, the greater the demand will be for the technology that can support it. As of this writing, Cisco is projecting global IP traffic to pass 1 trillion gigabytes for the first time. Currently, Verizon and AT&T are in a race to be the first cell phone provider to offer 5G service, which promises to be between 10 and 100 times faster than today's 4G LTE. Although the projected launch date for the technology is 2020, we can safely expect the push to transmit more information more quickly to continue well past that date.

But as with earlier advancements in communication, these increased capabilities will continue to disrupt the way business is conducted. Streaming music and video services cut into the market for CDs and DVDs. Online shopping permanently changed retail stores. As video conferencing quality improves, we can expect a lot more meetings to be done online rather than in person, saving countless dollars and man hours in travel. What other industries will be transformed?

The demand for instant access to all kinds of entertainment will continue to grow. But the increased sharing of movies and music across oceans and continents is also making the world much smaller. American and British productions are already hits all around the globe. I think we can expect those trends to move in the other direction as well, as people from multiple countries begin to partake in each other's favorite dramas, comedies, and thrillers.

What kinds of businesses will thrive in this increasingly connected world with higher and higher speeds of data transfer? What kinds of creative solutions will be needed to meet its needs? I think we will see increasingly bold ideas both to bring us greater connectivity and to make tremendous use of it.

2. Disease, Injury, and Aging

While I was writing this book, my mother had her hip replaced. What was once a major surgical procedure taking several hours and requiring weeks of bed rest is now in many cases a relatively minor outpatient procedure. Furthermore, the surgery is often robot-assisted, and after the initial incision the doctor doesn't actually have physical contact with the patient. The continual improvement in the materials used for joint replacement and the techniques and tools used for the procedure itself have made the process immensely more successful and much less of an ordeal for patients. With an aging population in many parts of the world, the need for these kinds of improvements will only grow.

In his book *The Guide to the Future of Medicine: Technology and the Human Touch*, author Dr. Bertalan Meskó describes the trends that are likely to shape our healthcare both in the short term and further down the road. In the short term, Meskó anticipates a growing number of games and phone applications that will help patients with chronic conditions as well as those recovering from illness and injury to follow the appropriate course of treatment and rehabilitation. He also sees the increasing amount of medical information available online as continually empowering patients to be equal partners with their healthcare providers. Likewise, he predicts the growing use of technology for remote diagnosis and treatment.

Closer to the science fiction-like realm, Meskó anticipates improved prosthetics—some of which may eventually be produced by 3-D printers—as well as fully functioning organs made of human tissue grown in a laboratory. Like many, he believes we will also have more personalized medicine informed by our increasing knowledge of genetics. As he puts it, "The truth is that there are only about 30 cases when personal genomics can be applied with evidence in the background according to the Personalized Medicine Coalition. As we move along this path, we will have more and more opportunities for using DNA analysis at the patient's bedside which should be a must have before actually prescribing drugs."[4] Robot-assisted medical procedures and improved sensors to monitor various bodily processes will likely change the way doctors are educated as well as the way medicine is practiced.

Further on the horizon, Meskó sees a greater role for artificial intelligence (AI) in medical decision-making, as well as increased use of virtual reality in medical training. Along with many others, he believes that microscopic robots will eventually be developed that are small enough to be injected into human beings to provide a variety of ways to treat and monitor disease. This trend will most likely lead to both mental and physical human enhancements made possible through technology.

Improved treatments and increased longevity also point to medical care moving toward preventative and wellness-enhancing measures. All these trends present numerous opportunities for boldly led companies to provide new products and services that most of us have only dreamed of.

3. Dealing with Information Overload

New technology has given us reams of data about processes and phenomena that were previously completely mysterious. We have cameras looking inside the human body, at the bottom of the ocean, and into the farthest reaches of the solar system. We gather data from sensors on windmills, inside oil pipelines, and on the bodies of birds and other animals. Our social media posts and digital fingerprints are gathered along with billions of others and analyzed to discern our movements, spending habits, and insurance needs.

This onslaught has already revolutionized the business world. Data mining—the practice of combing through large amounts of information in search of trends and predictions—is really just getting started. It has already led to radically different forms of targeted marketing; you've probably noticed ads for cold medicines appearing on your computer right after you searched for "cures for the common cold." The precision with which machines are able to predict human behavior will only increase, and speech and facial recognition technologies are likely to continue to improve as well.

But along with all the incredible opportunities that such data provides have come some new problems. First, all this information has empowered us to do more for ourselves, but this often carries a heavy cognitive burden. As author Daniel J. Levintin observes in his book *The Organized Mind: Thinking Straight in the Age of Information Overload*, "Thirty years ago, travel agents made our airline and rail reservations, salespeople helped us find what we were looking for in shops, and professional typists or secretaries helped busy people with their correspondence. Now we do most of those things ourselves. We are doing the jobs of 10 different people while still trying to keep up with our lives, our children and parents, our friends, our careers, our hobbies, and our favourite TV shows."[5]

Levintin further explains that instant messages, texts, emails, and other small interruptions—that often prevent us from sustaining concentration on a more difficult task—are like "candy" for the brain: full of stimulation but empty of nutrients. Each time the brain has to shift tasks, it burns more of the fuel needed to stay focused. Thus, such distractions are actually depleting the brain's resources, which can lead to a condition neuroscientists call cognitive overload. This causes us to become confused, disoriented, and raises the level of stress hormones in the blood stream.

Writing in *Harvard Business Review*, Paul Hemp explains, "Current research suggests that the surging volume of available information—and its interruption of people's work—can adversely affect not only personal well-being but also decision making, innovation, and productivity. In one study, for example, people took an average of nearly 25 minutes to return to a work task after an e-mail interruption."[6] According to the Information Overload Research Group, the wasted time costs the American economy nearly a trillion dollars in productivity every year.

Information overload presents two major challenges: the need to process large amounts of information quickly, and the need to determine which information is important in the first place. Unfortunately, the more information we are faced with, the slower we tend to process it.[7] In fact, research suggests we can only process a certain amount of information in one day, no matter how hard we try.

We can safely expect the technologies that filter information to continue to become much more sensitive and "smart," allowing us to decide what we see and when we see it. I think we are also likely to see increasing options that allow us to cut ourselves off to all information except emergency contacts for various periods of time, making it easier to concentrate on a demanding task. We may also see new software to help us organize and declutter our virtual lives.

Both consumers and businesses will be looking for ways to avoid missing vital information and to prevent making mistakes in their rapid-fire correspondence. They will look for better ways to skim or process written documents to get the main points without becoming bogged down with all the details. Those who can create visual short cuts such as infographics will be needed more than ever.

Lastly, the need for greater information security and privacy protection will only grow. Not only will people want ways to protect their financial and personal information, but they will likely want shortcuts to keep their personal and professional lives separate from each other. Bold minds that can find new solutions to these problems will undoubtedly be in demand.

Increased Automation

We have already seen an automation revolution in our lifetimes. From ATMs and automatic voice prompts within voicemail systems, to the mechanical arms assembling ours cars and computers, nearly every industry has been transformed by increased robotic precision and AI. There seems to be no end to what these amazing machines can do.

Automation, as many have observed, is a double-edged sword. In most cases we use it to extend our capabilities (think robot-assisted surgery) or to allow our brains to conserve energy so we can focus on more complex tasks (think calculator or computer-assisted design). But what happens when we become so dependent on the technology that our brains begin to lose the ability to perform certain tasks on their own? We've almost all become dependent on our calculators to help us with basic arithmetic and our phones to remember countless phone numbers. Now many are losing their ability to navigate a city with a map—since their GPS will do it for them—or to back up their cars without the rearview camera.

Automation also has a complex effect on the economy. On the one hand, it undoubtedly makes goods cheaper to produce and thus offers consumers lower prices. On the other, many lower-skilled workers may lose their jobs as machines improve to the point of being able to perform tasks better and cheaper than humans can.

This isn't always a zero-sum game, however. For example, the number of ATMs in the United States increased fourfold between 1980 and 2010, but the number of people employed by banks grew during this time as well.[8] The benefit to consumers was unmistakable; no one could have ever gotten cash from a bank at 2 a.m. before there was a machine to dispense it. Yet the banking industry itself also expanded, increasing the demand for more human workers.

But what about the automated kiosk that will soon take your order at the local fast food restaurant? The manager loves it, because it never makes a mistake and doesn't require health benefits, overtime pay, or a retirement fund. The customers may love the accuracy, but many might prefer to interact with an actual human being. For the moment, it seems uncertain where this trend will stop.

Advances in AI also mean that lower-skilled jobs are not the only ones at stake. Tasks that would have seemed unimaginable for a machine—flying planes and driving cars, for example—are already being performed by robots. In the immediate future, however, the overwhelming majority of jobs do not seem to be in jeopardy. According to a 2015 report

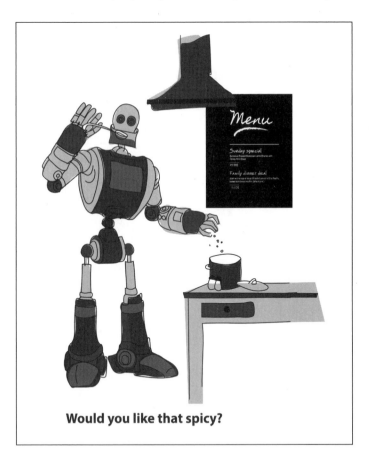

Would you like that spicy?

published by McKinsey Global Institute, entitled *Four Fundamentals of Workplace Automation*, at least in the short term, most jobs would be redefined rather than eliminated.

The authors explain that they believe very few occupations would become entirely automated, but instead, "certain activities are more likely to be automated, requiring entire business processes to be transformed, and jobs performed by people to be redefined. . . . More specifically, our research suggests that as many as 45 percent of the activities individuals are paid to perform can be automated by adapting currently demonstrated technologies."[9]

Even highly skilled workers such as doctors and executives engage in some activities that could be automated, according to the report. But human beings would still be necessary to provide supervision and make final decisions of consequence. Furthermore, greater automation will no doubt continue to improve working conditions and safety for human workers, as it has already done in many manufacturing jobs.

Tim O'Reilly—a technology advocate best known for popularizing the term "open source"—sees these trends affecting the nature of work itself. He notes that automation has affected how workers are allotted hours, with complex software programs now doing the job of shift managers. In his article *Workers in a World of Continuous Partial Employment*, he explains that the old way to handle uneven labor demand was to keep a "stable core of full-time workers to meet base demand" and a larger pool of part-time workers that could be called in to meet peak demand. But increasing regulations requiring expensive benefits for full-time workers incentivizes companies to keep everyone part time. O'Reilly elaborates that "sophisticated workplace scheduling software lets companies build larger-than-needed on-demand labor pools to meet peak demand, and then parcel out the work in short shifts and in such a way that no one gets full time hours."[10]

The current debate is whether workers being managed by such software should be treated as employees or as independent contractors. O'Reilly believes that traditionally run companies with employees could take a cue from what he calls "Next Economy" companies—like Uber or Lyft—that utilize independent contractors. Next Economy companies make the data from the shift management software available to everyone, which empowers more workers to set their own hours and work until their income goals are met.

Another growing challenge—since machines will certainly be increasingly utilized for entry-level work—will be teaching younger workers the skills they need to learn in order to enter the work force. After all, entry-level jobs do more than provide labor to accomplish a specific task. They teach younger workers how to stick to a schedule, follow instructions, navigate the authority structure of an organization, and so on.

There will be an increasing need to prepare younger workers—who lack skills and work experience—for full-time employment.

However far automation goes, human beings will never stop needing to connect with other human beings. We all grow tired of talking to machines, no matter how efficient they may be. The more tasks become automated, the more the human touch will become a highly prized commodity. Some businesses will undoubtedly be able to capitalize on the increasing rarity of human interaction in day-to-day transactions. Companies that can provide a superior customer experience will undoubtedly be able to flourish.

5. Meeting the Demands of the Bold New World

Increased interconnectedness, new ways to bring products to market, and exploding technology to make the cumbersome aspects of certain tasks much easier are already leading to a global surge in innovation. Yet according to a 2012 study by Adobe, there is a growing global creativity gap in most companies. Eight in 10 of the 5,000 adults surveyed (across five countries: the United States, the United Kingdom, Germany, France, and Japan) believed unlocking creativity was vital to economic growth, but only 25 percent of respondents felt they were fulfilling their creative potential.[11]

Increased creativity will be needed not only to advance technology and to create the new products and services that such technological advances make possible, but also to bring those products and services to ever-expanding global markets. The future workforce will need to be both digitally savvy and relentlessly bold-minded in order to keep up. Yet younger workers are notoriously disengaged. Many young people today show remarkable creativity when developing content for their social media accounts, but often do not apply that same creative energy in the workplace.

Companies will need people who are able to motivate and engage younger workers so that they can offer their full creative potential to the task at hand. This means in many cases that leaders will need to find ways to make work meaningful and important to those they employ. Teaching newer employees to tap into the right kind of motivation for work will arguably be just as important as helping them complete their assignments in a timely manner.

As technology increases so will the desire to expand human potential by finding ways to learn faster, perform better, and age more slowly. As we map more and more of the brain, advances in neuroscience and nanotechnology will likely enable our brains to interact directly with computers and artificial intelligence without a keyboard or mouse. Such changes will increase the gap between the computer literate and those without access to such technology, thus increasing the demand for educational services for those segments of the global population in need.

Lastly, the wise have noted for millennia that greater power does not make humans wiser or better. Growing technology creates ethical and moral dilemmas that have not previously existed. Before advanced life-support technology, including machines that help us breathe and help our hearts to beat, it was not necessary to create anything like an advanced directive. Martine Rothblatt, discussed in Chapter 7, has published *Virtually Human*, "a big-think manifesto on the rights of yet-to-be-created cyber-humans."[12] But there will be many more ethical issues raised by exploding technology that will require bold minds to address them.

Bold minds have been changing the world for millennia, and they will continue to do so for the foreseeable future. In the coming years, we will all find our imaginations stretched past what we ever thought possible. The future belongs not so much to those who can accurately predict what it will look like, but to those who can anticipate its problems and find the best ways to solve them.

Twelve

Power, Presence, and Well-Being

ONE OF MY FAVORITE movies is called "About Time," a romantic comedy starring British actor Domhnall Gleeson as the protagonist Tim, who learns that he can travel through time (under somewhat constricted conditions that prevent him from altering major world events and so on). Tim, a softhearted and likeable guy, initially uses this ability to repeat certain moments in his romantic life until he gets them "right." After a few missteps, he is able to settle down with the girl of his dreams.

Tim also tries his hand at righting a few wrongs for his family members and eventually uses his gift to spend more time with his dying father. Along the way, he finds that one of the best uses of time travel is to live each day twice, even when he doesn't want to change anything. He finds that he enjoys each day so much more the second time through, because he is no longer preoccupied with what he has to get done or worried about outcomes that he cannot control.

By the end of the movie, however, Tim has learned that he can actually choose to live each day only once but savor each moment as he did when he was living it for the second time. In a gentle, humorous way, the movie reminds us that the ability to cherish each moment is the essence of a life well lived.

The development of the mind is not a purely professional or even a purely intellectual pursuit. Everything we do to realize more of our brain's potential should ultimately be geared toward becoming the best version of ourselves that we can be and living the best life that we can. After all, what is the point of being deeply creative or even profoundly influential if we cannot enjoy our relationships and savor the time we are alive? Even becoming wealthy or famous is empty without a sense of peace and well-being.

Many thinkers have explored the tension between who we are and what we do. How much do we find our identity in our occupation? To what degree does the creation define the creator? At the end of the day, whatever our occupation, the most powerful creative energy flows out of who we are. It comes when we feel inspired and motivated. On a chemical level this means maintaining high levels of serotonin and dopamine and minimizing stress hormones like cortisol. On a spiritual level, it means we are centered and connected to what is most important to us.

Bold minds are not always found in the most aggressive or ambitious among us. They are found in those who can cultivate the right chemical balance in their brains. They are found in people who can strike the correct balance between what they do and who they are and between the needs of the moment and the needs of the future.

The ultimate goal of the theories and practices outlined in this book is not only to unleash the creative potential of each individual (and organization), but also to help us to live more deeply and more boldly for our own good and the good of those around us. In doing this, we each do our part to contribute to the bold new world on the horizon.

Let Go of the Old

The human brain is built to find ways to conserve energy. It does this by automating behaviors into habits. The advantage of this tendency is that we are able to go about our daily lives without concentrating intensely on mundane or routine tasks. Unfortunately, it also becomes incredibly easy to get stuck in unhelpful behavior patterns or in habits that were once necessary but outlive their usefulness.

This tendency to find comfort and ease in routine can also cause us to become subconsciously devoted to a business model or a product long after it becomes obsolete. Remember that it takes extra mental energy to examine our habits and assumptions critically to see if we are clinging to an idea or a practice that has outlived its time. But our ability to do so is vital to innovating successfully.

Our brains also naturally resist risk, because their primary purpose is to keep us alive. Success—far from making us bolder—often makes us even more risk averse. Once we have achieved something, we naturally become more concerned with protecting what we have than achieving something new.

It takes significant exertion of energy to prevent us from becoming prisoners of our own success. Wagon wheels, whale oil lamps, and dial-up internet were all extremely successful for a time, but then that time ended. Clinging to them longer didn't make them stay.

Becoming bound to an outdated or unhelpful idea or pattern of behavior almost always happens gradually, so that it often escapes our notice. We need to have regular checks in place to ensure that we are not unknowingly becoming too complacent or comfortable. We should also take daily steps to ensure we stay curious, open, and enthusiastic about learning.

The world is changing rapidly, and that change will only accelerate in the years to come. Accept that you (and your company) will not be the same in five, 10, or 20 years. Remember, Thanatos is not to be feared. He comes to carry off ideas, products, services, business models, and production and delivery methods when their time has come. Don't resist him, even if he comes for something you hold dear. Let go of old ways, and make room for the new.

Don't be Afraid of Risk

Anything bold and new, by definition, requires risk. But not all risks are created equal. Unfortunately, many people judge risk by their emotional reaction to an idea rather than by a rational evaluation. The difference between a good risk and a bad risk has little to do with how scary or safe the risk feels. The drastic cuts and subsequent purchases at Fujifilm were likely terrifying to all those involved. Yet they ensured the company's survival and eventual rebirth, while Kodak was laid to rest forever. On the other hand, Border's risk of building new stores probably felt comfortable; they were doing what they had done in the past to find success. Yet that decision was ultimately the nail in their coffin.

Of course from a very young age we are taught to be risk averse, because many of the risks we might take in childhood and adolescence could get us killed. Such risks are most often the product of immature brains and an undeveloped prefrontal cortex. Yet adults are not immune from foolish risk-taking. Just as there is no upside to not looking both ways before you cross the street, there are some business risks that are simply the result of carelessness, impulsiveness, or a failure to research all options thoroughly. Good risks are almost always the result of careful planning and calculation or putting oneself in a position to take advantage of an opportunity as soon as it presents itself.

Always remember to take into account the risk of not acting in a particular situation. Sometimes, doing nothing is the right decision, but other times it robs you of a vital opportunity to grow. Ultimately, too much hesitation can be worse than making a bad decision. The minds and companies shaping the future are not immune to mistakes. They are simply willing to move forward decisively and correct course when necessary.

Remember, your bold new idea could come in many forms. You could come up with innovative products and services, but you might also develop innovative improvements, productions, business models, marketing concepts, or customer experiences. Winning ideas can come suddenly or gradually. They can take weeks to develop or years.

You will never be able to innovate without risk, but you can evaluate it, minimize it, and account for it. Make sure your business plan prepares for mistakes and allows for course corrections. And then take a step to make it happen!

Take Care of Your Body, Your Soul, and Your Personal Relationships

Remember your mind is made better and bolder if it resides in a healthy body that is leading a healthy balanced life. A huge part of keeping a healthy chemical balance in the brain is eating well, staying physically active, taking in plenty of fresh air and sunshine, and getting sufficient sleep. Taking the time to ponder what you are thankful for before you go to sleep will greatly increase the quality of your rest and the subsequent benefit to your brain and body.

Work to effectively manage your four "energies": physical, mental, emotional, and spiritual—keeping life in balance whenever possible. Your spiritual energy can be more closely related to your creativity than you might think. All of us, as human beings, possess both strengths and weaknesses, shadow and light. To seek greater creative power, we must take the time to purify our motivations. Creativity and innovation pursued out of love, passion and generosity will soar much higher than what is pursued for fearful or self-serving reasons.

We must also make the effort to purge fear from our souls. Fear of failure, fear of rejection, and fear of the future all promote the wrong chemical balance for creativity. We must take the time to check ourselves for selfishness and egotistical motivations that can sometimes hide behind other things. Do you feel resentful when people don't give you credit for something? Would you have trouble welcoming a truly helpful innovation if it came from a competitor instead of from you? A truthful yes to either of these questions could be a sign that you aren't tapping into your best motivations. We all work with so much more passion and energy when we know we are working for the greater good rather than just for ourselves.

A balance between work and personal relationships is vital. Work, like any other activity, can be overdone. And if you habitually neglect your body and your relationships, you will soon fade, like a flower cut from a plant. Dysfunctional or troubled relationships will inevitably bleed over into the rest of your life and have a profoundly negative effect on your creativity. Get rid of toxic people and invest your time and effort into those you love. Even for very introverted people, healthy, loving relationships are really what life is about.

Care for Your Brain

Your brain is an organ, just like the rest of your body. It requires proper nourishment, exercise, and rest. Wandering thoughts, the inability to focus, and difficulty recalling information when you need it are all signs you may need to take better care of your most important organ.

Our thoughts, imaginations, preoccupations, and obsessions are what ultimately determine who we become. They shape the lens through which we see the world. You are in full control of your thoughts and where to direct your concentration, but you may need to work to be able to exercise this control effectively. Like training for a race or any other athletic endeavor, directing your concentration requires practice and discipline.

Meditation is excellent exercise for your brain. Whether it's Focused Awareness like Zen, Open Monitoring like mindfulness, or Self-Transcending like Transcendental Meditation, find a meditation practice that helps you accomplish your goals. These could include greater focus, a reduction in anxiety, or just a greater sense of peace and well-being. Whatever your personal objectives are, meditation can be a wonderful and easy way to care for your brain and keep it young.

Remember that creativity—in the bold mind model at least—is not something we do as much as it is something we receive. It isn't finite, it's boundless. It is not about generating the most ideas as much as it is about tapping into creative potential. It's deeply influenced by your subconscious as well as your conscious thoughts. Make sure you are mastering and nourishing your mind, so that it will yield the creative abundance you want.

Build Creative Momentum

Creativity is like a fire; it can grow and spread, or it can sputter and go out. Guarding your creative momentum—as in the success spiral we discussed in Chapter 4—is just as important as guarding your ideas. This does not mean avoiding failure at all costs, but rather taking care to process failure the right way. It is better to fail quickly and move on than to waste too much time in limbo over an idea or a decision.

You can't build momentum without motion, which means that you must take at least some of your "first creation" ideas all the way to "second creation" and to market. Too many immensely talented individuals spend so much time pondering possibilities that they forget to actually follow through. Even a moderately successful launch will teach you invaluable lessons and help you to plan more effectively for the next time.

Building momentum also requires reinvesting the ideas, money, and other resources you obtain back into the creative process. On the mental level this means creating positive reference points for future endeavors. On the practical level it means not sinking everything you have into the innovation of the moment, instead setting aside funds and time for the next innovation that you haven't thought of yet.

Challenge Your Brain to Grow

As we age, our brains can begin to slow down and even atrophy, but they do not have to. We can take steps every day to help our brains remain healthy and continue to form new neural connections. Remember that your current levels of knowledge, understanding, creativity, and even intelligence are not set in stone. Your brain can grow and improve until the day you die.

There are many ways to challenge your brain. Reading rigorous material on a variety of subjects and spending time with well-read and knowledgeable friends should be regular parts of the life of the bold mind. Remember that not all of your brain challenges need to be directly related to your work. Practicing a foreign language, a musical instrument, or learning any new creative skill can all be ways to encourage your brain to continue developing.

Remember to identify and work on any unproductive habits as well as minimize the distractions you face on a regular basis. In addition to finding an app or a planner that helps you organize your thoughts and tasks, many people benefit from developing a focusing ritual that helps them clear their heads. Also remember to schedule time into the day to think, write, and reflect on what you have learned.

Engage with the Disruptive

Whether it's offering a playfully sarcastic remark, visiting an ironic art exhibit or even catching a magic show in Vegas, allow time to engage with stimuli that disrupt your way of thinking. Stay curious and indulge your curiosity. Explore. Investigate. Along the way, embrace the constraints that you face in your endeavors, and treat them as roadmaps to innovation rather than roadblocks that prevent you from achieving your goals.

Experiment with techniques like synectics and case studies (described in Chapter 7) to disrupt your usual patterns of thinking. If you're feeling more adventurous, enroll in an improvisational theater class or try painting, sculpting, or music lessons. Remember none of these activities need to relate directly to your job or your other goals in life. Think of them as ways to stir up the contents of your brain so you can rearrange your reality.

Optimize Your Performance

Working to optimize your performance on a regular basis can involve several different techniques. As you prepare for an important event or presentation, keep the two "systems" (Kahneman's System 1 and System 2) of your brain in mind. Remember that peak performance—whether you are a professional golfer or a CEO—often involves less of System 2 and more of System 1. Just like athletes practice certain motions or reactions over and over—with both physical and mental repetitions—until they become automated, you can use both actual rehearsal and specific visualization to prepare.

While you are practicing or learning, remember to keep your brain in the "learning zone," where you are sufficiently challenged but not overwhelmed. If you're feeling particularly bold, try an immersion technique, where you remove all the "easier options" from your plate and force yourself to master a new skill. Take care when practicing any visualization to keep the images and outcomes realistic. Spending time fantasizing about a future you have no clear way to achieve will not get you any closer to making it happen. Specific, detailed visualization, however, can become like a preview of important things to come.

Travel to the Future

Most people take the time to think about where they would like to be in five or 10 years, but remember that you can actually allow your mind to spend time in the future. Even if you don't participate in a full Time Machine Experience as discussed in Chapter 8, you can still allow yourself to visualize the ideal, short-term future realistically and then retrace your steps (or come up with the large action steps) that took you to that desirable place.

It can be very easy in the chaos and stress of everyday life to lose sight of what an ideal future entails. But it is so important that we keep the images, vocabulary, and even the emotions of those possibilities before us on a regular basis. Too many people have allowed themselves to be caught up in the mundane and relatively unimportant tasks that consume their days, while decades of their lives have slipped away.

Rethink Your Professional Relationships

So much innovation comes not only from individual creativity, but also from productive collaboration. Are you getting the most you can out of your professional relationships? Are you approaching these relationships with the right attitude? Allow yourself to approach your professional partnerships with a mindset of a shared ideal future. Move forward with the vision that there is more than enough for both parties to prosper and thrive.

A Final Thought on Well-Being

Unlike Tim, we don't get a second or third try at each day. But we can approach each day with the energy, focus, and attitude of enjoying every moment to the fullest, creating a better world for ourselves, for those around us, and for society as a whole.

NOTES

Chapter 1

1. Eric Wagner, "Five Reasons Eight Out of Ten Businesses Fail," *Forbes* (September 9, 2013).
2. Avi Dan, "Kodak Failed by Asking the Wrong Marketing Question," *Forbes* (January 23, 2012).
3. Carlos Castaneda, *The Teachings of Don Juan: The Yaqui Way of Knowledge* (Ballantine, 1973), 7.
4. Clarissa Pinkola Estes, *Women Who Run with the Wolves* (Ballantine, 1996), 324.
5. Sean Silcoff, Jacquie McNish, and Steve Ladurantaye, "Inside the fall of BlackBerry: How the smartphone inventor failed to adapt," *The Globe and Mail* (September 27, 2013).
6. Estes, *Women*, 324.

Chapter 2

1. Paul Johnson, *A History of the American People* (Harper Perennial, 1999), 781.
2. Kathy Chin Leong, "Google Reveals its Nine Principles of Innovation," *Fast Company* (November 20, 2013).
3. Ibid.

4. Jillian D'Onfro, "YouTube Still Doesn't Make Google Any Money," *Business Insider* (February 25, 2015).

Chapter 3

1. Baba Shiv, "How do You Find Breakthrough Ideas?" *Insights by Stanford Business* (October 15, 2013).
2. Tania Lombrozo, "The Truth About the Left Brain/ Right Brain Relationship," *National Public Radio* (December 2, 2013).
3. Agnes de Mille, *The Life and Work of Martha Graham* (London: Random House, 1991), 264.
4. Simon N. Young, "How to Increase Serotonin in the Human Brain without Drugs" *Journal of Psychiatry and Neuroscience* (November 2007).
5. Ibid.
6. Richard Alleyne, "Playing a Musical Instrument Makes You Brainier" *The Telegraph* (October 27, 2009).
7. Joanne Cantor, "Sleep for Success: Creativity and the Neuroscience of Slumber" *Psychology Today* (March 15, 2010).
8. Joshua Wolf Shenk, "The Power of Two" *The Atlantic* (July/August 2014).
9. Stuart Firestein, *Ignorance: How It Drives Science.* London: Oxford University Press, 2012.
10. Carolyn Drebin, "Questions for Bruce Nussbaum," *Rotman Management* (Fall 2013).
11. Graham Brown and Markus Baer, "Protecting the Turf: The Effect of Territorial Marking on Others' Creativity" *The Journal of Applied Psychology* 100 (November 2015).
12. Patricia Stokes, *Creativity from Constraints: The Psychology of Breakthrough.* New York: Springer Publishing Company, 2005.

13. Emmet Malloy, "The White Stripes: Under the Great White Northern Lights" *Three Foot Giant/Woodshed Films* (2009).

Chapter 4

1. Ray Williams, "Why Don't My Positive Affirmations Work?" *Psychology Today* (October 14, 2012).
2. Carol Dweck, *Mindset: The New Psychology of Success,* (Random House, 2006), 16.
3. Rob Asghar, "Why Silicon Valley's 'Fail Fast' Mantra is Just Hype," *Forbes* (July 14, 2014).
4. "Welcome to Bermuda: the Airbus-ORACLE TEAM USA innovation partnership advances with co-location of engineering personnel" *Airbus.com* (August 4, 2015)
5. Adam Bryant, "Good C.E.O.'s are Insecure (and Know It)" *New York Times* (October 9, 2010).
6. C. Otto Scharmer. *Theory U: Leading from the Future as it Emerges,* (Berrett-Koehler Publishers, 2009).
7. Michael M. Grynbaum, "Starbucks Takes a Three-Hour Coffee Break," *New York Times* (February 27, 2008).

Chapter 5

1. James Allen, *As a Man Thinketh,* (Tremendous Life Books, 2009).
2. Carolyn Gregoire, "Easily Distracted by Noise? You Might Just Be a Creative Genius" *Huffington Post* (March 10, 2015).
3. Jack L. Groppel, *The Corporate Athlete: How to Achieve Maximal Performance in Business and Life* (Wiley, 1999).
4. Tony Schwartz and Catherine McCarthy, "Manage Your Energy, Not Your Time" *Harvard Business Review* (October 2007).

5. Heather A. Wadlinger and Derek M. Isaacowitz, "Fixing our Focus: Training Attention to Regulate Emotion" *Personality and Social Psychology Review* (February 2011).

6. Tracy Cheung, Marleen Billebaart, Floor Korese and Denise De Ridder, "Why are people with high self-control happier? The effect of trait self-control on happiness as mediated by regulatory focus" *Frontiers in Psychology* (July 8, 2014).

7. Daniel Kahneman, *Thinking, Fast and Slow* (Farrar, Straus and Giroux, 2011).

8. Eckart Tolle, *The Power of Now: A Guide to Spiritual Enlightenment* (Namaste Publishing: 2004), 49.

9. Daniel Goleman, *Focus: the Hidden Driver of Excellence* (Harper, 2014).

10. Bruce Lee, *Tao of Jeet Kune Do* (Black Belt Communications, 2011).

11. William M. Kelley, Dylan D. Wagner, and Todd F. Heatherton, "In Search of a Human Self-Regulation System" *Annual Review of Neuroscience* (April 30, 2015).

12. Jonah Lerher, "Don't! The Secret of Self-Control" *New Yorker* (May 18, 2009).

13. Laura Rabin, Joshua Fogel and Katherine Nutter-Upham, "Academic Procrastination in College Students: The Role of Self-reported Executive Function" *Journal of Clinical and Experimental Neuropsychology* (Vol. 33 Issue 3 2011).

14. Marcus Tullius Cicero and Margaret Graver, *Cicero on the Emotions: Tusculan Disputations 3 and 4* (University of Chicago Press, 2002).

Chapter 6

1. Stephanie Liou, "Neuroplasticity," *Hopes: Huntington's Outreach Project for Education at Stanford University,* (June 26, 2010).

2. Wendy Zuckerman and Andrew Purcell, "Brain's Synaptic Pruning Continues into Your Twenties," *New Scientist* (August 17, 2011).

3. David Brooks, *The Social Animal* (Random House, 2011), 49.

4. Lois Romano, "Riding Accident Paralyzes Actor Christopher Reeve," *Washington Post* (June 1, 1995).

5. Karen Weintraub, "Stimulation Restores Some Function for Four Paralyzed Men," *USA Today* (April 8, 2014).

6. Traci Pederson, "Nerve Growth Factor Implant for Alzheimer's Shows Promise," *Psych Central News* (February 14, 2015).

7. "The Science: The Growth Mindset" *Mindset Works* *www.mindsetworks.com/webnav/growth-mindset -research.aspx*

8. Ibid.

9. Ibid.

10. Carl Zimmer, "The Brain: Why Athletes are Geniuses," *Newsweek* (April 16, 2010).

11. Ibid.

12. *http://thinkexist.com/quotation/i_never_hit_a_shot-not _even_in_practice-without/295577.html*

13. Geoff Colvin, *Talent is Overrated: What Really Separates World-Class Performers from Everybody Else* (Portfolio, 2010).

14. Heather Kappes and Gabriele Oettingen, "Positive Fantasies about Idealized Futures Saps Energy," *Journal of Experimental Social Psychology* (February 2011).

15. Brooks, *Animal*, p. 41

16. Bjorn Rasch and Jan Born, "About Sleep's Role in Memory," *Physiological Reviews* (April 2013).

17. A. M. Wood, S. Joseph, J. Lloyd, and S. Atkins, "Gratitude Influences Sleep Through the Mechanism

of Pre-sleep Conditions," *Journal of Psychosomatic Research* (January 2009).

Chapter 7

1. Richard Gray and Alexandra Genova, "How Einstein Changed the World with His Theory of General Relativity . . . and Why You Would be Literally Lost Without It," *Daily Mail* (November 25, 2015).
2. J. K. Witt and T. E. Dorsch, "Kicking to Bigger Uprights: Field Goal Kicking Performance Influences Perceived Size," *Perception*, Vol. 38, pages 1328–1340; 2009.
3. Richard Wiseman, *The As If Principle: The Radically New Approach to Changing Your Life*, (Free Press, 2013).
4. Ibid. p. 108.
5. Neely Tucker, "Martine Rothblatt: She founded Sirius XM, a Religion and a Biotech. For Starters . . ." *Washington Post Magazine* (December 12, 2014).
6. Edmund L. Andrews, "FCC Plan for Radio by Satellite," *New York Times* (October 8, 1992).
7. Amina Elahi, Haley Hinkle and Cheryl V. Jackson, "Martha Stewart Trumped by Manufactured Organs, Everlasting Love . . ." *Chicago Tribune* (October 15, 2015).
8. Melissa Dahl, "Elizabeth Gilbert on the Link Between Creativity and Curiosity," *New York Magazine* (September 23, 2015).
9. Neely Tucker, "Martine Rothblatt: She founded Sirius XM, a Religion and a Biotech. For Starters . . ." *Washington Post Magazine* (December 12, 2014).
10. Dawn M. Ehde, Tiara M. Dillworth, and Judith A. Turner, "Cognitive-Behavioral Therapy for Individuals with Chronic Pain," *American Psychologist* (February-March 2014).
11. "Talk Therapy May Reverse Biological Changes in PTSD Patients" *Elsevier* (December 3, 2013).

12. George M. Prince, "How to be a Better Meeting Chairman," *Harvard Business Review* (January 1969).
13. Natalie Wolchover, "NASA Gives Up On Stuck Mars Rover Spirit," *Space* (May 24, 2011).
14. Li Huang, Francesca Gino, Adam D. Galinsky, "The Highest Form of Intelligence: Sarcasm Increases Creativity for Both Expressers and Recipients," *Organizational Behavior and Human Decision Processes* (July 17, 2015).
15. Ibid.
16. J. Katz-Buinincontro, "Does Arts-based Learning Enhance Leadership? Case Studies of Creativity-oriented Executive Institutes" *American Education Research Association* (2005).
17. Jesse Scinto, "Why Improv Training is Great Business Training," *Forbes* (June 27, 2014).
18. Ibid.

Chapter 8

1. "Self-Determination Theory," http://selfdetermination theory.org/theory/
2. Brigid Schulte, "Harvard Neuroscientist: Meditation Not Only Reduces Stress, Here's How it Changes Your Brain," *Washington Post* (May 26, 2015).
3. Ibid.
4. Jan Hoffman, "How Meditation Might Boost Your Test Scores," *New York Times* (April 3, 2013).
5. Jeanne Ball, "How Meditation Techniques Compare. Zen, Mindfulness, Transcendental Meditation and more" *Huffington Post* (September 22, 2010).
6. Alice G. Walton, "Transcendental Meditation Makes A Comeback, With The Aim Of Giving Back," *Forbes* (April 27, 2015).
7. Laura Cadman "What Is NLP?" *www.anlp.org/what -is-nlp*

Chapter 9

1. B. L. Rayner, *The Life of Thomas Jefferson, with Selections from the Most Valuable Portions of his Voluminous and Unrivalled Private Correspondence* (Boston, Lilly, Wait, Coleman and Holden, 1834).
2. Benjamin Radford, "Synchronicity: Definition and Meaning," *Live Science* (February 4, 2014).
3. Ohio State University, "Both Liberals and Conservatives Have Anti-science Biases, Study Finds," *Psy Post* (February 10, 2015).
4. Dr. Bruce Lipton, "Are You Programmed at Birth?" *Heal Your Life* (August 17, 2010).
5. "World Bank Development Report 2015: Mind, Society and Behavior," p. 62.
6. Scott Barry Kaufman, "The Real Neuroscience of Creativity," *Scientific American* (August 19, 2013).
7. Scott Barry Kaufman and Jerome L. Singer, "The Creativity of Dual Process 'System 1' Thinking," *Scientific American* (January 17, 2012).
8. Humphrey Carpenter, editor, *The Letters of J.R.R. Tolkien,* (no. 142 to Robert Murray, December 2, 1953).
9. Charlotte Seager, "How the Subconscious Mind Shapes Creative Writing," *The Guardian* (April 7, 2015).
10. Ibid.
11. Paul C. Holinger, "Self-Awareness: Transition from Infant to Toddler," *Psychology Today* (November 19, 2012).
12. Dan P. McAdams, "The Psychology of Life Stories," *Review of General Psychology* (2001, Vol. 5, No. 2, 100-122).
13. Ibid.
14. Todd Henry, *The Accidental Creative: How to be Brilliant at a Moment's Notice,* (Portfolio, 2013).

15. James Allen, *As a Man Thinketh*, (Tremendous Life Books, 2009).
16. *http://thinkexist.com/quotation/to_visualize_is_to_see _what_is_not_there-what_is/331347.html*
17. Theresa Amabile, "How to Kill Creativity," *Harvard Business Review* (September-October 1998).

Chapter 10

1. Heidi K. Gardner, "When Senior Managers Won't Collaborate," *Harvard Business Review* (March 2015).
2. "Wikipedia: Statistics" https://en.wikipedia.org/wiki /Wikipedia:Statistics
3. Amanda Neville, "Five Signs Your Partnership is Doomed," *Forbes* (March 15, 2013).
4. Heather Perlberg, "Stocks Perform Better if Women Are on Company Boards" *Bloomberg* (July 31, 2012).

Chapter 11

1. "Bell Labs and Innovation: The Organisation of Genius," *The Economist* (April 21, 2012).
2. Jon Gertner, *The Idea Factory: Bell Labs and the Great Age of American Innovation*, (Penguin Books: 2012) 234-235.
3. Gernter, *Idea Factory*, 4.
4. Bertalan Meskó, *The Guide to the Future of Medicine: Technology and the Human Touch*, (Dr. Bertalan Meskó: 2014).
5. Daniel J. Levintin, *The Organized Mind: Thinking Straight in the Age of Information Overload*, (Dutton: 2014).
6. Paul Hemp, "Death by Information Overload," *Harvard Business Review* (September 2009).
7. Ibid.

8. James Bessen, "Toil and Technology," *Finance and Development* (March 2015, Vol. 52, No. 1).
9. Michael Chui, James Manyika and Medhi Miremadi, "Four Fundamentals of Workplace Automation," *McKinsey Quarterly*, November 2015.
10. Tim O'Reilly, "Workers in a World of Continuous Partial Employment," *Medium* (August 31, 2015).
11. Russell Brady and Lisa Auslen, "Study Reveals Global Creativity Gap: Universal Concern that Creativity is Suffering at Work and at School," *Adobe* (April 2012).
12. Neely Tucker, "Martine Rothblatt: She founded Sirius XM, a Religion and a Biotech. For Starters . . ." *Washington Post Magazine* (December 12, 2014).

INDEX

Index

Index

ABOUT THE AUTHOR

DESCRIBED BY BUSINESS LEADERS as an advisor, mentor, coach, and highly trusted business partner, Scott Cochrane's passion is to help organizations move toward revolutionary thinking. He is widely known for challenging the status quo, asking "why not?" and igniting a spirit of bold thinking and accelerated growth in companies around the globe. Scott's "Bold Mind" approach has convinced presidents, CEOs, senior leaders, and executive boards of organizations, including Amadeus, Cisco, Danone, HP, ING, Pepsico, Shell, and Tech Data, to engage his speaking, coaching, and advisory services. He works internationally and lives in Boynton Beach, Florida.